The Redemption of Tragedy

I0895607

SUNY Series, Simone Weil Studies
Eric O. Springsted, editor

The Redemption of Tragedy

The Literary Vision of Simone Weil

Katherine T. Brueck

State University of New York Press

The following passages have been quoted from *Sophocles: Three Tragedies*, trans. H. D. F. Kitto (Oxford University Press, 1962). By permission of Oxford University Press.

From *Antigone*: (1) lines 440–450
(2) lines 979–983
(3) lines 891–901; 910–916
From *Oedipus the King*: (1) lines 835–43
(2) lines 1308–22; 1349–54
(3) lines 1451–64

Published by
State University of New York Press, Albany

© 1995 State University of New York

All rights reserved

Printed in the United States of America

No part of this book may be used or reproduced
in any manner whatsoever without written permission
except in the case of brief quotations embodied in
critical articles and reviews.

For information, address the State University of New York Press,
State University Plaza, Albany, NY 12246

Production by Christine Lynch
Marketing by Nancy Farrell

Library of Congress Cataloging-in-Publication Data

Brueck, Katherine T., 1951–
The redemption of tragedy : the literary vision of Simone Weil / Katherine T. Brueck.
p. cm. — (SUNY series, Simone Weil studies)
Includes bibliographical references.
ISBN 0-7914-2281-X (acid-free). — ISBN 0-7914-2282-8 (pbk.) (acid-free)
1. Weil, Simone. 1909–1943. 2. Tragedy—History and criticism. 3. Philosophy in literature. 4. Literature—Religious aspects.
I. Title. II. Series.
PN1892.B78 1995
809'.916—dc20 94-9152
CIP

10 9 8 7 6 5 4 3 2 1

For my students

...Nothing almost sees miracles
But misery.

—*King Lear*

Wherever there is affliction, in any age or any country, the cross of Christ is the truth of it.

—Simone Weil

Table of Contents

Acknowledgments

I would like to express my gratitude to Professor Eric O. Springsted for his encouragement and helpful advice at crucial stages of manuscript preparation.

I would also like to acknowledge my debt to Dr. Ann Begley, both for suggestions concerning style and for insights regarding the definition of important terms.

The Mount St. Mary's College Professional Development Fund has granted me regular release time from teaching duties in order to facilitate work on this book. I appreciate their generosity.

Finally, I would like to thank my husband, Dr. Donald Brueck, for the insights of a general reader. I am also indebted to him for unfailing moral and technical support. Above all, I would like to thank Don for countless hours of devotion to our two young children, Emily and Heidi, without which this book could not have been written.

Abbreviations

Abbreviations of Simone Weil's works will appear as follows in the text and in the notes:

Écrits de Londres	EL
First and Last Notebooks	FLN
Gravity and Grace	GG
Gateway to God	GTG
Intimations of Christianity among the Ancient Greeks	IC
Notebooks	N
Oppression and Liberty	OL
Poèmes suivis de Venise Sauvée	PVS
Science, Necessity and the Love of God	SNL
Seventy Letters	L
Simone Weil Reader	SWR
Two Moral Essays	TME
Waiting for God	WG

Series Editor's Preface

Simone Weil had an important relationship to literature from early on, and not just because of the formative influences of her family and her *lycée* education. Already in the 1930s, before it had occurred to many philosophy professors to do so, she was teaching philosophy by means of literary works, finding it far more helpful in getting her point across than many other, more traditional, means. It is therefore not surprising that in her writings she frequently turned to comment on literary subjects. Why exactly she taught this way, and why she spent a great deal of time on literary topics, especially in her later writings, is of particular interest. At one point in her notebooks, she comments, "The Gospel contains a conception of human life, not a theology." This is at least to say that it can be positively misleading to state certain important truths in strictly objective and clearly defined propositions; many truths breathe only within the context of lived experience. They have to be seen in order to be entertained and comprehended. Literary works are therefore crucial, unique places to understand those truths.

It is with this in mind that it is particularly helpful that Professor Brueck's study appears, being the first full-length study of Weil's approach to literature. But, as Professor Brueck herself points out, there is also another reason to pay attention to Weil's literary ideas. For not only is Weil distinctive in using literature to think philosophically and religiously; she also employs a distinctive approach to literature itself, especially tragic literature. This, Professor

Brueck argues, is an unabashedly "supernatural" approach, an approach in which tragedy not only retains its tense moral elements but in which that tension is also seen as redemptive. This approach of Weil's to tragedy has been little noticed, although it well deserves to be. Thus, in Weil, we find a surprising alternative to present theories of tragedy as well as finding that new avenues are opened up in discussions of the relation of religion and literature, and even what possibilities exist for reading life itself religiously in the twentieth century.

Eric O. Springsted

Introduction
Tragedy and the Supernatural

The Redemption of Tragedy: The Literary Vision of Simone Weil departs from the usual kind of work devoted to Simone Weil (1909–43). It is a study of Simone Weil neither as a religious or political thinker, systematic or otherwise, nor as a contemporary spiritual or revolutionary figure.[1] In this book I will discuss very specifically Simone Weil's ideas on tragedy. I believe that Weil's thoughts on tragedy contain much that contributes both to the understanding of tragic art generally and, more particularly, to the interrelation between tragedy and Christianity.

This interpretation of tragic drama by the light of Weil's metaphysics exemplifies a supernaturalist approach to literature. Contemporary literary theory, as twentieth-century literature itself, rarely evinces a transcendent orientation. This fact may be traced to the influence of modernism. A modernist regards skeptically any affirmation of a supernatural reality. Modernist skepticism contains both a rational and an irrational dimension. The naturalist, for example, maintains a rational or scientific outlook, whereas the atheistic existentialist, or the nihilist, sustains an irrational point of view. Both kinds of thinker, however, regard supernaturalism as the product of fancy or wish fulfillment.

The naturalist contends that the entire knowable universe is composed of natural objects. As a natural object himself, the human being exists entirely within the spatiotemporal and the causal order. The human being ought not legitimately to go outside the system of natural objects for explanations of what takes place within nature. Indeed, in principle, nonnatural explanations may be replaced by natural explanations. Thus, because the human being exists entirely in the order of nature, he does not have a soul, nor, therefore, does he have contact with a religious or spiritual realm beyond nature. Consonant with the naturalist's view is the scientistic outlook: The only legitimate mode of knowledge is scientific. Concomitantly, the universe at large is regarded as amoral in character.[2]

Phenomena which naturalists must sometimes regard as unexplainable in scientific terms become the predominant focus of a second kind of modernism, also antisupernaturalist. This species of thought, often either existentialist or nihilistic, conceives reality as irrational, rather than rational, in character. The modern irrationalist, contrary to the naturalist, rejects a scientific explanation of human existence.

For the purposes of studying tragedy, the most significant ramification of the modernist view concerns the problem of suffering. The title character of Henrik Ibsen's *Hedda Gabler* or the Mannon family in Eugene O'Neill's *Mourning Becomes Electra* are exclusively products of natural forces: heredity and environment. Suffering crushes the characters of these naturalist dramas, leaving them hopeless. Similarly, although the irrational modernist abandons the naturalist's scientific interpretation of human behavior, certain existentialist plays such as Albert Camus's *Caligula*, or an absurdist (nihilistic) drama such as Samuel Beckett's *Waiting for Godot*, depict suffering also as intrinsically meaningless.

The uplifting though painful experience of the classical tragic hero lies outside the realm of possibility for the protagonist of a modernist drama. In opposition to the modernist view, the classical tragedian posits the existence of supernatural forces. Whereas the supernatural does not alleviate suffering yet, often it imbues pain with meaning. Relationship with a divine power enables the protagonists of classical tragedies such as Aeschylus' *Seven against Thebes* or Shakespeare's *Hamlet* to acquiesce nobly to an otherwise wretched existence.

Again, this book constitutes a study of tragic drama in the light of Simone Weil's metaphysics. Weil's essential outlook is that of mystical Christian Platonism. Thus, the supernaturalist basis of this book depends on Weil's conception of the connection between tragedy and Christianity and between tragedy and Platonic thought.

Simone Weil regards the genius of the Christian religion in terms of its attitude toward suffering. More specifically, she conceives the Christian view of human wretchedness in a fashion comparable to that of classical tragedy: "The extreme greatness of Christianity lies in the fact that it does not seek a supernatural remedy for suffering, but a supernatural use for it" (*GG*, 132). Like the classical tragedian, and the modernist playwright, Weil also regards suffering as a central, unalterable human experience. For Weil, however, as often for the tragedian, affliction can afford meaning on a level above the rational.

Tragedy is customarily regarded as more nearly akin to a modernist than to a traditional religious point of view. It is also perceived as rather Aristotelian than Platonic in spirit.[3] (Plato's work, of course, contains the philosophical roots of a supernaturalist outlook.) The tragic perspective of a mystical Christian Platonist, such as Simone Weil, points up the limitations of the prevailing view.

The majority of contemporary writers on tragedy, like Aristotle himself, secularize tragedy, thereby ignoring—or, at best, marginalizing—a central element of tragic experience: the supernatural.[4] Simone Weil, contrarily, suggests that major tragedies in the classical tradition presuppose a fragile but authentic link between suffering innocence and an apprehension of the transcendent. According to the world's religions themselves, only suffering of an innocent kind—whether technically 'guilty' or not—can ultimately yield religious intuition. Although a transcendent realm is knowable not by reason but only through an experience of the whole being—a phenomenon we call "pain"—yet the supernatural may be said to have objective reality apart from human existence.[5] From this perspective, then, an affirmation of the supernatural is not the work of wish fulfillment or fantasy, as the modernist asserts.

By focusing our thoughts on the relationship between suffering and supernatural knowledge, Simone Weil's discussions of the classically tragic help to revise a popular but unfounded view that faith in the supernatural is the product of an escape mentality. As Plato proposes, as the religious traditions and the greatest classical tragedies manifest, far from offering an "opiate" or an "escape," a supernatural good can authentically be known only through the necessary. Only the rough, thick hands of suffering and evil can lift for us the fine veil that conceals a good without condition or flaw.

When certain major classical tragedies are considered from a Weilian perspective, these dramas may be read in earnest hope of new insight. A Weilian reading reveals that the religious traditions may regard these plays as genuinely sacred works of art. As the first chapter of this study suggests, one may discount as inauthentically sacred a work of art which, while claiming to evoke or enshrine a supernatural reality, at the same time disclaims a central connection with moral categories, that is, with good and evil. From the perspective of the religious traditions, at least, such works of art can be regarded only as sophistical. An interest in a moral law whose foundation is divine marks certain classical tragedies as authentically sacred poems, in opposition to works of poetry which are written in a romantic spirit. The romantic poet or literary critic, while claiming knowledge of a "spiritual" or "supernatural" reality, at the same time either ignores or blurs the distinctions between good and evil. This moral void is usually the result of identifying, rather than distinguishing between, a natural and a supernatural realm. The romantic simply equates the moral with the didactic, and therefore dismisses moral concerns as being unworthy of an artist's attention. Despite his pretension to writing sacred poetry, his dismissal of art's ethical dimension disqualifies the romantic's artistic vision as being a religious vision in any genuine sense.

The supernatural reality of the great religions, unlike the romantic's value-neutral one, is good. This Good is Absolute.[6] The mystical faculty, an "inner eye," may apprehend a supernatural reality when intense pain completely overcomes the ego, the source of self-centeredness, the fountain of evil. Intuition of the supernatural is not accessible, then, to a morally neutral eye such as that of the romantic. Additionally, because the Good which the mystic ultimately apprehends is suprarational rather than rational, the kind of knowledge to which the mystic attains is inaccessible also to a moral eye attached to reason alone, a vision such as that of the strictly rationalist Christian.

In general terms, the suprarational may be distinguished from the rational and the irrational as a phenomenon which lies above rather than on, or below, the level of reason. Whereas the rational, when separated from the scientistic viewpoint, may affirm moral qualities, it does so without transcending them. The irrational, on the other hand, necessarily overlooks or denies the very categories of good and evil themselves. Unlike either the morally rational or the irrational, then, the suprarational transcends even as it asserts a distinction between good and evil. The truths to which an authentically sacred work of art points, as the moral laws it enshrines, are both suprarational as well as rational. It follows that any critic who lacks an intuition of the suprarational cannot, except accidentally, identify an authentically sacred work of art. Neither the irrationalist nor the moral or amoral rationalist, therefore, can be said to provide a reliable identification of the sacred. To this state of affairs, one which I believe hampers insight into masterpieces of classical tragedy, the light of mystical Christian Platonism may profitably be directed. Again, this beam of light may be found in the thought of Simone Weil.

Weil, a Platonist with a mystical Christian cast, regards the cross of Christ as the essential suprarational reality. As a mystery, a good suprarational in kind, the cross reconciles or transcends, even as it acknowledges, distinctions between good and evil. As the first two chapters of this book establish, the Christ's cross constitutes the cornerstone of Weil's

Christian Platonist theory of tragic art. It is therefore advisable to explain here what the cross of Christ itself signifies for Simone Weil.

According to Christian belief, generally, the cross of Christ constitutes a sacrificial act of atonement for the world's sins. This sacrifice Christ, the Son of God, offered to the Father, creator of the world. The atonement, or redemption, enables any human being who believes in the efficaciousness of Christ's crucifixion to receive divine forgiveness for his sins and also release from their deleterious effects.[7]

When Weil herself speaks of the cross, she focuses less on the joyous results of Christ's having been crucified than she does on the sufferings Christ himself endured in order to make the divine mercy effective. In this Weil is truly a mystic, for the mystic's goal, in the Western religious traditions, is not to win favor for herself from God but rather to know and to love him for himself alone.[8] For Weil, a Christian mystic, then, attaining knowledge of God is possible only by obtaining knowledge of Christ's sufferings. This knowledge itself can be veritable only if it is experiential rather than abstract. Pure love of God, then, for the Christian mystic, a love which is identical with perfect knowledge of God,[9] can be attained only by experiencing the same kind of torment that Christ suffered on the cross. This species of torture itself includes a braving of anguish in the same spirit as Christ's own endurance.

Weil suggests that a human being may experience a suffering comparable to that of Christ's cross when she is smitten by "affliction," a consummate suffering—physical, social, psychological, and even moral (*WG*, 134, 122). Affliction, always imposed against one's will, constitutes a kind of living death. This is a condition which causes a person, like the crucified Christ, to feel abandoned not only by human beings but by God as well. The desolate soul endures her torment in a Christlike spirit when she refrains from seeking consolation for her misery in bitterness or anger or hatred but, rather, sustains an attitude of gentle love. A love for the good which triumphs even in degradation resembles the love of Christ for the Father during the time when Christ suffered the most intensely: the moment when Christ believed that the Father had abandoned him to the sins of the world on the cross (*WG*, 126–27). Christ's most intense misery was unconsoled precisely because Christ bore his anguish in an attitude of perfect love. From the mystical Christian viewpoint of Simone Weil, then, only by maintaining an attitude of love for the good in utter misery can one come to know Christ; only thus can one come to know God. Tragic art, then, beyond any other, may be called sacred, for it alone enshrines the courageous spirit of a love for the good which endures in the depths of affliction.

The very order of things, according to Weil, enables the human being to share in Christ's cross. The Father creates the world through the mediation of the crucified Son. As St. John says, the Lamb himself was slain from the foundation of the world.[10] Thus, the very universe itself can be thought to be made in such a way that it mysteriously cooperates with human beings to achieve spiritual perfection.

If the world may be said to bear the stamp of Christ's cross, then the creation enables the same kind of spiritual victory that classical tragic drama describes. Though tragic drama focuses on the problem of human misery, yet, in opposition to modernist plays, suffering contains an intrinsic meaning. An uplift results from the description of a human soul which, rather than being crushed by, rises above, the adversity imposed by the exterior world.[11] This triumph often occurs as a result of painful contact with a transcendent realm. The loving afflicted soul Weil describes offers an instance of inner victory in outer defeat comparable to that of the classical tragic hero. Affliction, the most extreme form of adversity, enables the highest possible spiritual victory, from a Christian perspective: participation in the cross of Christ. Thus, as chapter 2 proposes, Weil indicates a profound harmony between the outlook of classical tragedy and the Christian vision in its mystical dimension.

In order to illustrate concretely how Weil's mystical Christian view of tragedy differs from modernist conceptions of this artistic form, chapters 3 and 4 discuss four specific classical tragedies: Sophocles' *Antigone* and Shakespeare's

King Lear, and Sophocles' *Oedipus Rex* and Racine's *Phèdre*. As we will see, when they are regarded in the light of religious mystery rather than through the lens of modernist philosophy—as is more commonly done—these tragedies appear to answer the challenge posed by the many contemporary opponents of Christian tragedy. The chief objection to the possibility of harmonizing the tragic with the Christian perspective is the modernist and the rationalist Christian belief that divine justice does not exist in tragic art. From a Weilian perspective, a justification of God's ways to man may be derived not only from the tragic portrayal of innocent suffering (*Antigone* and *King Lear*) but even from the tragic dramatization of compulsory wrongdoing (*Oedipus Rex* and *Phèdre*)—this latter in contradiction of much contemporary ethical theory.[12] The mystery of Christ's cross sanctifies innocent and degrading misery alike.

A specifically Christian theodicy may be derived from tragedy of crime as well as tragedy of calamity, then, when a Christian interpretation of the tragic rests, as it does throughout this book, on the mystical facet of Christianity (the cross of Christ) rather than on its exoteric (i.e., its rational or legalistic) dimension. At the same time, however, a tragic theodicy can not be understood outside the context of moral law, a context which the romantic and his philosophical allies regularly fail to discern in tragic art.

The romantic's mistaken notion of the supernatural as irrational rather than suprarational is one example of a variety of views which, in one way or another, deny the existence of any reality that exists above the level of reason. One of these views, as we have seen, is the naturalist. The specific family of thought to which I refer, however, conceives reality in irrational rather than in rational terms, whether in a sentimental vein (the romantic) or in a less emotional one (the nihilist). With the minor exceptions of pragmatism and structuralism—both of which bear a resemblance to the naturalist viewpoint—I use the word *modernism* in the following chapters to connote an outlook that both denies the suprarational and conceives reality in irrational rather than in rational terms. This orientation, like the naturalistic one, either underplays, ignores, or denies the existence of moral categories.

Thus, besides offering specific illumination concerning tragic drama, *The Redemption of Tragedy* hopes to point up, more generally, the fruitfulness of a supernaturalist literary viewpoint. Currently, the supernaturalist outlook is without voice within literary conversation. As this book's conclusion implies, a placing of the transcendent interpretation of literature alongside the two orientations which currently prevail—the nihilistic and the ideological—could stimulate a debate comparable to that which occurred between the sophists and Socrates in fifth-century B.C. Athens. Currently, the reign of poststructuralist literary theory makes the open-mindedness necessary for this kind of discussion impossible. The modernist outlook, in its irrational and its rational modes, unfairly dominates the literary scene.[13]

Even contemporary discussions explicitly devoted to the interrelation of literature with religion lack a supernaturalist orientation. With the assistance of Simone Weil, I hope now to help raise the conversation concerning poetry and the sacred to the transcendent level proper to it.

Notes

1. The best scholarly study of Simone Weil as systematic Christian thinker is Eric O. Springsted's *Christus Mediator: Platonic Mediation in the Thought of Simone Weil* (1983); Springsted's *Simone Weil and the Suffering of Love* (1986) makes Weil's Christian metaphysics accessible to broad audiences without diluting the profoundness of her vision. The most recent book-length study of Simone Weil, Thomas Nevin's *Simone Weil: Portrait of a Self-Exiled Jew* (1991), historicizes and psychologizes Weil's thought. Unfortunately, the book thereby undermines Weil's Christian metaphysics and also her mysticism.

A reliable study of Weil's political thought and influence may be found in Lawrence A. Blum and Victor J. Seidler's *A Truer Liberty: Simone Weil and Marxism* (1990).

The definitive critical biography of Simone Weil is Simone Pétrement's *La vie de Simone Weil* (1973).

Readers interested in a full Weil bibliography are encouraged to consult J. P. Little's *Simone Weil: A Bibliography* (1973) and *Simone Weil: A Supplement* (1979). More recent bibliographical information is available through the American Weil Society. This society is the American division of a French organization founded in 1974, l'Association pour l'Étude de la pensée de Simone Weil.

2. This definition of naturalism I draw from two sources: (1) Arthur C. Danto, "Naturalism," in the *Encyclopedia of Philosophy* (1967); and (2) M. H. Abrams, "Realism and Naturalism," in *A Glossary of Literary Terms* (1993), p. 175.

3. The ascendancy of Aristotelian over Platonic thought in discussions of tragic art is easily explained. In *The Republic*, Plato criticizes the poets of his time, including the tragic poets, on both moral and metaphysical grounds. Aristotle, on the other hand, devotes an entire work to the sympathetic study of poetry: *The Poetics*. This work is itself devoted primarily to the analysis of tragedy. For the relevant texts, including reliable comment, see Walter Jackson Bate (ed.) *Criticism: The Major Texts* (1970), pp. 13–49.

The tendency to assume that tragic art conforms to a modern skeptical rather than to a traditional religious point of view can be best seen, perhaps, in the contemporary debate about whether or not a Christian tragedy is possible. In this debate, religious thinkers commonly disavow the tragic vision; concomitantly, thinkers who defend a tragic outlook spurn a religious point of view. For a list of thinkers who disbelieve that a Christian tragedy is possible, see ch. 2, n. 15.

"Classic" readers of Greek tragedy who feel the need to protest against modern skeptical misreadings of ancient plays offer further evidence that thinkers today tend to associate the tragic outlook with a skeptical rather than a religious viewpoint. Note, for example, the following comments by scholars of Greek tragedy:

1. "Sophocles' religion is not merely a kind of top-dressing, a general suffused piety, but a controlling element, something that shapes the action quite as much as the human characters and motives do. It is not an idea which is congenial to an essentially rationalist and irreligious age like our own" (H. D. F. Kitto, *Sophocles: Dramatist and Philosopher* (1958), p. 22).

2. "Just as in life a complex situation may force us to take sides and to pass judgments, so in Sophoclean tragedy the conflicts make the same demand. And when this happens we are particularly likely to be led astray by modern notions" (C. M. Bowra, *Sophoclean Tragedy* (1947), p. 8).

3. According to Herbert Weir Smyth, moderns are reluctant to acknowledge Aeschylus' ultimate faith in the justice of Zeus. Rather than attend the existing fragments of the Promethean trilogy, they prefer to equate Aeschylus' vision with that of the *Prometheus Bound* alone. "Moderns are loath to draw within the circle of their vision the *Prometheus Unbound.* Truncated as is this trilogy, these atomists would cast out of sight even the poor remnants of that tragedy in order that they may preserve unimpaired the image of an unshaken and defiant will supported only by the justice of its cause" (*Aeschylean Tragedy* (1924), p. 120).

4. Charles Whitmore suggests that, in opposition to superficial modern approaches to tragedy, "the study of the supernatural in tragedy is not that of an arbitrarily limited field, but the tracing of a necessary connection between the two terms" (*The Supernatural in Tragedy* (1915), pp. 349, 356).

5. The painful quality of the route to religious knowledge is described variously by students of the world religions. It is referred to as (1) self-naughting (Huston Smith, *The Religions*

of Man (1986), pp. 43, 141, 242, 272, 295, 350, 443–44); (2) purgation (Evelyn Underhill, *Mysticism* (1974), pp. 17, 222); (3) the death of an old self, preceding a new birth (Mircea Eliade, *The Sacred and the Profane* (1959), pp. 187, 190, 192, 197, 201); (4) contact with a "wholly other," a *mysterium tremendum*, felt initially in its power, only later in its goodness (Rudolph Otto, *The Idea of the Holy* (1970), esp. pp. 17, 105); (5) the opening of a third or inner eye (William Johnston, *The Inner Eye of Love: Mysticism and Religion* (1978), esp. pp. 9, 38).

6. Seyyed Hossein Nasr, *Knowledge and the Sacred* (1989), p. 135.

7. William J. Wolf, "Atonement: Christian Concepts," in *Encyclopedia of Religion* (1987), vol. 1, pp. 495–98.

8. On the selflessness of the mystic's love of God, see Underhill, *Mysticism*, p. 85; Johnston, *Inner Eye of Love*, p. 28.

9. See ch. 2, n. 13 on mystical knowledge as a function of love.

10. The phrase "the Lamb slain from the foundation of the world" occurs in the New Testament, in Revelation 13:8 (authorized version). Simone Weil often quotes this verse (see, e.g., *WG*, 145; *NB*, 222, 246, 380).

11. See ch. 2, n. 33.

12. Martha Nussbaum and Stanley Hauerwas offer important examples of a relatively recent interest in the problem of moral tragedy among philosophers and theologians. Both authors believe that discussing the possibility of compulsory wrongdoing threatens to upset generally accepted views concerning the moral nature of human beings. Nussbaum approaches the problem from a modernist perspective, Hauerwas from a Christian point of view (Hauerwas, *Truthfulness and Tragedy* (1977); Hauerwas, *A Community of Character* (1981); Nussbaum, *The Fragility of Goodness: Luck and Ethics in Greek Tragedy and Philosophy* (1986)).

13. Huston Smith makes a plea for an opening of the academic mind to include a suprarational perspective, in the field of religion itself. See Smith's 1989 plenary address to the American Academy of Religion, printed as "Postmodernism's Impact on the Study of Religion," *Journal of the American Academy of Religion* (Winter 1990), p. 668.

Chapter One

The Sacramental Poetics of Simone Weil

Simone Weil brings the perspective of the world religions to the problem of the interrelation between poetry and the sacred, in opposition to a chorus of modernist thinkers who view the interrelation of literature and religion from a philosophical or an anthropological point of view. Because Weil's worldview, including her poetics, rests on the outlook of the great religions, I will refer to Simone Weil throughout this book as a "traditionalist." The religious traditions assert the existence of a supernatural, as well as a natural, realm. Tradition (religion) constitutes a mediation between the two.[1]

A voice distinct from other traditionalists in our century, Weil views the interplay between art and religion specifically through the lens of mystical Christian Platonism.[2] Simone Weil draws from this religious philosophy a new and compelling theory of sacred art, an idea which, in its essence, constitutes a theory of Christian tragedy. Hitherto, the debate concerning the possibility of harmonizing the Christian and the tragic visions of the world has lacked the underpinning of a theory of tragedy which is specifically Christian. From the perspective of the religious traditions, such a theory must furnish as artistic paradigm an act of the divine creation which tragic art might be said to imitate.[3] I propose that the thought of Simone Weil supplies such a concept of the creation, as of religious art.

Weil's idea of Christian tragedy can become accessible only if one understands first both the Platonic and the mystical Christian dimensions of her underlying concept of religious art. This fact constitutes the rationale for the present chapter.

As suggested above, critics today tend to study the relationship between literature and religion from one of two fundamental perspectives: modern or traditional. Modernists discuss this interrelation outside of the context of any particular religious tradition, including the Judeo-Christian. They do so necessarily since they reject as untenable the foundation of all the greater (and the lesser) religions, the existence of a transempirical reality, a reality inaccessible to the faculties of sense. The modernist tends, therefore, to ground his idea concerning religion and literature in philosophy or in anthropology rather than in religion itself. A modernist may, for example, follow the lead of a contemporary philosopher, such as Martin Heidegger, who offers poetry as revelation of a god who is neither beyond nor separate from nor superior to the phenomenal world.[4] Or in an anthropological rather than in a philosophical mode, a modernist may regard literature not as a substitute for traditional religion, as the Heideggerian critic does, but rather as a barometer, like the religions, of *Zeitgeist*. The anthropological or pragmatic critic regards the study of religious and literary texts as valuable for its ability to uncover and illuminate the value systems of diverse cultures.[5]

As I have suggested, the epistemological premise on which thinkers, like Simone Weil, rest their discussions of the commonality of literature and religion is that of the world religions. Thus, a belief in the existence of a supernatural reality undergirds Weil's view of the relationship between these two disciplines. For the traditionalist, such as Weil, ultimate reality is apprehended not through the senses, the only means to knowledge the empiricist admits as valid, but through a faculty known as "the eye of the heart" or "the eye of faith." This inner or third eye is described by those familiar with the esoteric or mystical dimension common to the great religions. The esoteric facet of religion is the secret or hidden dimension from which supernatural knowledge is derived.[6] Without the existence of this supernatural reality, phenomenal reality itself would neither be nor mean. The report of fundamental religious experience contained in scripture, and the continuing affirmation of mystical encounter, bear witness to the existence of a supernatural realm.[7]

From a traditional point of view, Simone Weil's insights into the mystical dimension of Christianity provide a sacralizing impetus to contemporary discussion of the relationship between literature and religion. This impetus, it would seem, has been sorely lacking in treatments of the subject, particularly in the United States.[8] From her intimate experience of the mysteries of the Christian faith, in particular, Weil draws a view of art that is sacramental in a sense which goes contrary to modernist conceptions of so-called religious art. Weil's view of art is sacramental not in the Heideggerian, essentially romantic, sense of the word, redolent of a holiness "immanent" in all things empirical. According to the romantic view, the natural and the "supernatural" are identified: This identification simply brackets the problem of good and evil. Weil's view of art, on the other hand, is sacramental in the traditional sense of the term, furnishing a rare and special kind of mediation between a natural and a supernatural realm. This mediation is ordinarily understood in Western civilization as a bridging between man and God. A harmonizing principle is required precisely when a natural and a supernatural realm are regarded not as identical but rather as distinct realities. To romantic monistic philosophy, therefore, Simone Weil opposes a limited or mediated dualism, a philosophy compatible with the outlook of the religious traditions.[9] A dualistic philosophy of this kind not only allows for but necessitates moral distinctions.

Weil, a Platonist, regards great art as performing an authentically religious function. Simone Weil follows Plato's conception when she proffers sacred art as a form of mediation between a natural and a supernatural realm. Weil's idea in this respect opposes the romantic immanentist notion of spiritual art, which, in opposition to the religious traditions, makes no distinction between the divine and the human.[10] As we shall shortly discuss, also in the vein of Plato, Weil soundly denounces the modern romantic litterateur who assumes a prophetic stance despite his skepticism regarding supernatural mystery as the religious traditions confess it. Weil continues in a Platonic mode when she opposes a reduction of religion or religious literature to a mere function of social reality, a cultural phenomenon, lacking an orientation toward the supernatural.

Although Weil is scarcely alone in her opposition to philosophical or secular discussions of the interrelation between literature and religion,[11] her particular import lies in her having developed, in the manner of Plato, a cosmogony which may serve as the model of a work of artistic creation which is spiritual in a traditionalist's sense. Weil's cosmogony is rooted in the central mystery of Christianity: the cross of Christ. Her particular idea of the creation as an act performed through the mediation of Christ's cross provides a model of artistic creativity which the tragic artist may be said implicitly to imitate. Thus, Weil's conception of the world's origins lays the foundations for a mystical theory of Christian tragedy.

For any traditionalist, of course, including Simone Weil, modernist, secular discussion concerning the religious quality of certain kinds of literature is of strictly limited value, if not positively harmful. The traditionalist asserts the primacy of religious truth, a truth which avows the unity and the supremacy of a Good which is absolute or eternal. She therefore regards the value of literature, as of all else, in light of that truth.[12] The modernist, on the other hand, does not accept the validity of sacred knowledge as the religious traditions confess it. He therefore tends to believe no significant boundaries between literature and religion exist. The modernist either places religious and literary texts side by side, as it were, on the same level of value, or he offers the one as a substitute for the other. The modernist thereby suggests that these two kinds of writing are not only of equal value but even interchangeable.

One of the most prolific and influential critics of religion and literature in America in recent years, Nathan Scott, may be taken as a suitable representative of one modernist orientation in the field, an orientation which may be called "romantic" or "aesthetic."[13] In his mature work, Scott is concerned to emphasize the 'religious' approach to literature in opposition to structuralist and deconstructionist literary criticism. These latter, recent, tendencies in literary theory bring to a logical solipsistic or nihilistic conclusion the earlier tendency of the New Criticism to discuss a poetic text without relating it to the real world.[14] In diametrical opposition to those who would subvert the relationship between poetic language and reality, Scott offers poetry as the only genuine means of understanding reality in its fullness and in its truth, that is, religiously.

Indeed, Scott suggests that the poet must substitute for the priest or prophet in the modern world. As a modernist, Scott believes that the perennial wisdom contained in the common thought of much of the theology and the philosophy of the past has become "ossified."[15] Because it is dependent on a belief in supernatural reality, this body of so-called knowledge is untenable. It is useless to anyone who subscribes to the modern, predominantly empiricist, mentality. Scott suggests that the death of traditional religion does not signify the demise of the sacred dimension of human existence, however. The poet, he asserts, can now supply the means to a truer and gentler 'piety' than any orthodoxy could ever offer. The creative artist can teach a sense of 'enthrallment' before the particular things of the world which an outworn and world-denying supernatural religion had only caused to go unnoticed, unappreciated.

In *The Poetics of Belief*, for example, Scott looks to several major nineteenth- and twentieth-century thinkers for support for his concept of the poet as prophet in the modern world. Each of these persons suggests, in some way, that the average human being lacks the poet's sensitivity to the enchantment or wonder of things and thus needs the poet in order to be awakened to the existence of the holy in the world around him. (None of the persons Scott cites subscribes to a traditional religious vision, at least not in his most creative periods.)

Thus, Scott lauds these particular ideas regarding poets and poetry: (*a*) Samuel T. Coleridge's theory of the secondary imagination, according to which the poet possesses a unique capacity to renovate the world of everyday for the 'lay' person; (*b*) Matthew Arnold's belief that though, from a modern or scientific point of view, the tenets of the Christian faith are meaningless phraseology or *Aberglaube*, yet poetry, including biblical poetry, when considered as poetry alone, can in its own way 'name the holy'; (*c*) Walter Pater's urging that the layman learn from the Renaissance artist to burn always with a gemlike flame and to approach the world in an authentically spiritual manner, that is, in an all-embracing attitude of openness or *disponibilité*; (*d*) George Santayana's belief that since, according to the empiricist mentality, the realm of matter is the only possible object of reverence, the highest activity in life is the activity which poets do best, that is, in Whitmanesque phrase, to have business with the grass; (*e*) Wallace Stevens's assertion that the poet alone, because he can reach things in their pristine reality through a process of artistic 'decreation', can offer 'fresh spirituals' to a desacralized world; and, finally, (*f*) Martin Heidegger's idea that the poet is a shepherd of Being, a namer of the holy, teaching us, as no one else can, how to revel in the particularity of things.

At times, Scott can speak in an appealing way of the poet's special function. He talks charmingly of the poet as a person who, in Heideggerian terms, promotes an attitude of *Gelassenheit*, or letting be,[16] before the things of the world. The poet's gentle regard for nature opposes a technological spirit of domination. And yet, despite the superficial appeal of his thought, it becomes quickly apparent that what Scott offers as a religious function for literature is actually a purely aesthetic one. What is lacking in each instance of 'poetic holiness' is a basis for a discrimination of values. From the point of view of the religious traditions, this lack can only bespeak a religious vision which is false. No religion which omits an ethical content can be veritable.[17]

The replacement of human nature by physical nature as the locus of the holy, particularly, bespeaks an evasion of moral categories. The tendency to regard Nature, rather than the eye of faith or the eye of the heart, as the locus of spiritual encounter was first begun on a grand scale by the Romantic poets. Scott often looks to these writers for support for his premises.[18] The Romantic holds up as an ideal an enthrallment before the things of the world without distinction. Comcomitantly, he infuses with charm the notion of *disponibilité* or openness before all the experiences of life. These aesthetic ideals may prove to be helpful for an artist who seeks to produce an appealing work of literature. However, to offer this attitude as a religion, as the basis for guiding human life and revealing ultimate truth, can legitimately be called an instance of sophistry. The romantic ideal is a principle which, if carried out, not simply in fiction but actually in life, results not in a spirit of reverence, as a critic like Scott maintains, but rather in nihilism.[19] Moreover, a true devotion to the things of the world inevitably results in some process of discrimination and, therefore, in an attitude of commitment in some form. This disposition Scott's ideal of *disponibilité* or openness precludes.[20]

Scott, however, scarcely stands alone when he offers as a religious what is in essence an aesthetic view of life. This proclivity may be seen as an instance of the confusion of religion with magic in literary circles which stems from the time of Romanticism. The tendency came to a height in European symbolism in the later nineteenth and early twentieth centuries.[21] It is the lack of ethical discrimination which above all distinguishes a magical from an authentically religious orientation. These two attitudes can be mistaken for each other, however, because of a common concern with the "spiritual" or the "supernatural." Traditionalists themselves do not confuse the two concepts, for they, unlike the romantics, do not identify the natural with the supernatural realm. Simone Weil is no exception, for, as we shall see, she articulates a view of spiritual art which, while claiming, like the romantic view, to be rooted in a vision of ultimate or spiritual truth, yet simultaneously holds the distinctions between good and evil at its core. This, in part, may explain her peculiar attraction to tragedy in the classical tradition, a tradition which consistently maintains a moral, and often supramoral, conception of human life.[22] As future chapters will show, the classical tragic tradition itself modernist critics have "aestheticized" or "de-moralized."

Romantic modernists, then, allow aesthetics to impinge on the territory of religion, to the point of claiming the function of religion for itself. Other modernists place religion side by side with poetry, disallowing any tendency to subordinate the latter to the former. This is an attitude foreign to all the religious traditions.

This second kind of equalizing approach to the study of literature and religion may be called the "cultural" or "pragmatic." In this instance, not the enthralling or the beautiful but rather the social or the useful is offered as the chief value of human life and, therefore, as the barometer for all criticism of the relationship between literature and religion. Like Nathan Scott, Giles Gunn, for example, speaks of faith in the existence of a supernatural reality as being both outworn and untenable.[23] Gunn, a pragmatist, does not, like Scott, offer literature as a substitute for revealed religion (though he allows for the possibility of doing this). Gunn, rather, views the study of the relationship between religious and literary texts as a form of cultural studies. Gunn thus regards the unique capacities of both poetic and religious writings to reflect the value systems of various times and cultures as the source of their continued claim to attention in a post-Christian age.

For his ideas concerning the interrelation of religion and literature, Gunn draws not primarily on the immanentist and therefore essentially romantic premises on which Scott bases his own work; American pragmatism, rather, is the source of his inspiration. Gunn follows consistently the pragmatic maxim that what works—that is, whatever helps one to adjust to his environment—is true: The meaning and truth of ideas is their cash value.[24] Thus, as Gunn himself points out, the pragmatist does not ask, What is real, as opposed to apparent? Nor does he ask, What is true, as opposed to false? The pragmatist asks, rather, What difference does it make to think one way or another about what is real or true?[25] The basis for this belief concerning what constitutes the appropriate philosophical question is a scientistic outlook: skepticism concerning the ability to attain legitimately to any truth which is transempirical or transcultural in kind.

For Gunn, the pragmatist, then, religion is not a means of revealing eternal reality or perennial wisdom. Religion, rather, is a reflector and shaper of culture. The pragmatist assumes, as does any empiricist, that there is no reality which transcends the social or cultural sphere. Indeed, Gunn suggests there is general agreement among scholars who study both disciplines that the common point between literature and religion is that both are 'makers of meaning.' Thus, Gunn implies very clearly that the one subject is of no greater or lesser value than the other.[26]

For Gunn, then—as, interestingly, for the sophist in the time of Socrates[27]—there is no realm of authority that is not culturally derived.[28] There is only biosocial reality. Gunn insists that religion is only one cultural form among others.[29] On these grounds, any traditionalist who objects to this view (as she must) he accuses of "theological imperialism."[30] In this critique of the traditionalist outlook, Gunn is consistent with the evolutionary perspective of the American pragmatist William James, for whom all facts of human existence as facts are of equal interest, including both religion and irreligion.[31] As a further consequence of his pragmatic premise, then, Gunn claims that the proper subject of the critic of religion and literature is not only the rise of religion in a certain culture but, also, of equal interest, its subsequent decline. Not surprisingly, Gunn cites a scholarly study of what he regards as the incipient demise or secularizing of Christianity in Romantic poetry as an example of the study of literature and religion at its best.[32]

The pragmatic empiricist shares with the romantic the conviction that each religion is a passing phenomenon, a function of history. Though a religion fulfills a need at a certain time, it contains no eternal truth.[33] This relativist attitude toward religion undergirds, for example, Heidegger's idea of the holy, a notion Scott quotes approvingly. Heidegger looks to the Romantic poet Hölderlin for knowledge of the divine. From this poet, Heidegger—and, Heidegger believes, all of humanity—learns that the condition of the modern scientific world is a condition of spiritual dearth. The gods who once were believed in have disappeared, and new gods have yet to make themselves known. Thus, Heidegger speaks of "the No-more of the gods that have fled and the Not-yet of the god that is coming."[34] It is, apparently, this—essentially modern—concept of the spiritual as the creation of human history that explains Gunn's allusion to Christianity as something outworn, as "the same stale game."[35] Similarly, Gunn refers to the confining of the study of literature and religion to the Judeo-Christian tradition as provincialism. Predictably, based on his relativist premises, Gunn makes this latter objection without reference to, much less on behalf of, other religious traditions.[36]

For Gunn, as for Scott, faith in a transempirical reality is something primitive.[37] Like Scott, however, Gunn also betrays a fundamental misunderstanding of the great religions themselves. He does not do so by mistaking an aesthetic for a religious view of reality (except in passing), but he offers as a peculiarly modern mentality what is, in its deepest sense, traditional. Gunn suggests that religious experience for primitive man involved worship of what the primitive believed to be another realm. The enlightened modern man, on the other hand, regards the "transcendent" other not as another realm, not as a reality beyond the self, but rather as a mode of access to change within the self.[38] This statement unfortunately betrays a lack of knowledge.

For the traditionalist, ultimate reality is at one and the same time completely other and the heart of the self.[39] Far from lacking an interest in psychology, the traditions hold what is known as a "two-self" psychology. According to the traditional interpretation of human personality, an old self needs to die so that a new one can be born. This is the sole authentic route to inner peace, though it involves pain. Indeed, the whole idea of catharsis in literature may be, and has been, seen in these, essentially mystical, terms.[40] Simone Weil's own ideas on tragedy may serve as an important reminder of this fact.

Gunn, then, suggests that ordinary literature serves a religious end in itself rather than being subject to evaluation in the light of scriptural texts. Like the human being himself, literature, as religion, is a maker rather than a reflector of meaning. It is this shared capacity to create fictions that enable human beings to endure which puts literature and religion—that is, nonscriptural and scriptural texts—on the same level of value. The traditionalist, on the other hand, asserts that art is never something autonomous. The value of a literary work is always viewed in light of the ultimate reality revealed in scripture. Absolute reality only scripture describes as well as human language can describe it. On this central point, then, the pragmatic view of the relationship between religion and literature is at least in no danger of becoming confused with the traditional.

It is important to point out, however, that the romantic empiricist, like Scott, shares with the traditionalist the view that art, rather than being an end in itself, serves an end beyond itself. The romantic and the traditional approaches to the relationship between literature and religion need, therefore, to be clearly distinguished. A confusion between them, based on this shared point, is possible.

For Scott, as for the traditionalist, it is the purpose of poetry to reveal ultimate or spiritual reality. For Scott, however, the ultimate, or the holy, is wholly immanent in the things of the world. A special, a poetic, eye discerns its existence. Ultimate reality, for the traditionalist, however, is not only immanent but transcendent as well, the transcendence being insisted upon.[41] This dualistic view contradicts the monism of Scott or any immanentist going back to Schelling and Hegel. From a traditionalist perspective—and, indeed, from the point of view of any intelligent person—without a sacred reality transcendent to and distinct from the phenomenal world, it makes no sense to say that that reality dwells also in the world. Without the transcendent, there is nothing to be immanent, and one is left, as we see Scott is left, with simply a heightened way of talking about empirical reality itself. Thus, from a traditional perspective, though a poet may be able to attain knowledge of the holy, this poet must be not a poet only but a genuine mystic as well.

It is by means of the philosophical monism which underlies the romantic point of view that the aesthetic dimension of the human experience can and does become confused with the religious. This confusion, in turn, makes possible the idea that religion and literature, rather than retaining their own spheres and boundaries, are interchangeable. The romantic's particular way of using major terms, such as 'religion,' 'transcendent,'[42] and 'sacramental,' perpetuates the problem.

According to the traditionalist outlook, in opposition to the romantic one, religious art performs the function of mediating between the transcendent or the sacred and the natural or the profane. Sacred art is "a revelation from that Reality which is the source of [the religious] tradition[s] and the cosmos; sacred art, then, has a sacramental function."[43] Fundamentally, sacred literature, specifically, then, is the poetry contained in the scriptures and religious myths themselves or poetry which otherwise reveals the mysterious, supernatural truths scripture and myth contain.[44] The romantic modern surrenders the concept of sacramentalism because he disbelieves in a transempirical reality. He therefore also disavows sacred knowledge and a mediating principle between the sacred and the profane. Unfortunately, while surrendering the concept of sacramentalism, he yet retains the term. According to Scott, for example, the entire world is a "sacramental" universe; this sacramental aspect only the poet has the capacity to reveal.[45] For Scott, Pater's ideal of unconditional openness before the experiences of the world is a form of "sacramentalism."[46] And, again, for this critic, all created things are indwelt by grace and by holiness. Scott speaks of the power of the "sacramental" principle within Christianity itself to break down all partitions between the sacred and the quotidian.[47]

What Scott offers as a religious principle here is not simply an aesthetic but also an atheistic principle. This is perhaps nowhere made clearer than in the similarity between Scott's use of the term *sacrament* and the use made of this word by Ludwig Feuerbach, the famous pupil of Hegel who is credited with being the first major philosopher to collapse theology into anthropology. In *The Essence of Christianity*, Feuerbach utters a common atheistic cry that a No to God is a Yes to man. Yet he couches this idea in terms which are themselves religious. In the section to which I refer, Feuerbach alludes apparently to the Christian sacrament of the Eucharist, a sacrament which commemorates the redeeming act of the crucifixion.[48] This religious mystery Feuerbach, a materialist philosopher, must wholly reject. Yet Feuerbach asserts, "Water, bread and wine are by their very nature sacraments....Therefore let bread be sacred for us, let wine be sacred, and also let water be sacred. Amen![49] The traditional (and original) idea of sacrament stands in diametrical opposition to this modernist sense that everything belonging to the world of man, because it belongs to man, is holy or sacramental. Indeed, for a materialist, like Feuerbach, everything human is more "holy" and more "sacramental" the more completely man is thought to have created God and not the other way around.

From a traditionalist viewpoint, a sacrament is that which mediates the presence and the power of the divine.[50] Far from being an expression of the entire human experience, a sacrament is a means by which the Christian may turn from the pressing distractions of the things of creation and the structures of society toward a dimension of his experience which is supreme though hidden. A sacrament mediates the presence and the redeeming power of Christ.[51] Sacraments are the particular means, within Christianity, whereby the supernatural may touch the natural realm, acting as a function of divine grace.[52] For Simone Weil, herself, as for any authentic Christian, a sacrament is a means of making real contact between the soul and God (*GTG*, 58). Unless the sacred is perceived, as it is perceived in the religious traditions, to be transcendent in essence, the idea of making contact with the transcendent, the idea of having both the need for, and the possibility of procuring, special ways of knowing and communicating with the divine becomes an irrelevancy. For this reason, in instances where the sacred is not regarded as transcendent, it would seem that, from the point of view of the religious traditions, certainly, the word "sacrament" should not be used. When it is used in such an instance, the effect is to give an air of religiousness to something which is in fact atheistic.

When, then, the traditionalist speaks of sacred art as serving a sacramental function, she means that art of this kind is a means, through the knowledge it conveys, of putting a person into contact with supernatural or sacred reality. This reality the Western mind understands as God. The sacramental function of art, from a modernist perspective, really has no meaning. Talk of this kind serves the purpose of lending a certain air of importance to art—a kind of defense mechanism, perhaps, in a scientific culture—and even again a sense of religiousness to something which is, in fact, atheistic.

As a traditionalist, Simone Weil holds art in less high a regard than Scott, who views art as a happy replacement for religion. She also esteems art to a lesser degree than Gunn, who contends that art serves a function equivalent in kind and quality to that of religion. In this attitude Weil closely follows Plato, a thinker whom traditionalists call their own[53] and whose concept of sacred art may serve, generally, as an example of the traditionalist conception in opposition to the modern. Since Plato's theory of art contains the seeds of

Weil's own ideas on the subject, a discussion of Plato's views will serve a double purpose of contrasting the modern with the traditional position and serving as a propaedeutic for Weil's own contribution to the discussion regarding the interrelation between religion and literature.

From a traditional perspective, Plato's is not simply a human philosophy but the result of divine inspiration.[54] From this viewpoint, whenever there is a revival of Plato, there is hope for the rediscovery of sacred knowledge.[55] When Plato's thought is restored in conjunction with the Christian message, the suprarational or mystical, the essential or original, elements of Christianity have a chance to be reborn.[56]

Plato regards all matters from a supernatural perspective. He views art with suspicion, therefore, because art imitates the phenomenal world. Already, then, it becomes apparent that, from a Platonic perspective, art will not be regarded as existing on the same level of value as religion. Art tends to fasten a person's attention and his affections onto the things of the world rather than to detach him from them. Thus, art obstructs the path to knowledge of a deeper and truer reality than the physical world outside, that is, knowledge of the spiritual kingdom both beyond and within.[57] For Plato, therefore, art is apt to hinder, rather than to help, a human being's quest both for ultimate knowledge and for inner freedom. The soul's search for the absolute, as described symbolically in Plato's allegory of the cave,[58] entails a tearing away from the things of sense, a demolishing of one's material—including, often, materialistic—values and a movement toward that which alone is real or eternal. This pulling away, this moving away from illusion toward a knowledge of what is true, identified by Plato with what is good and what is beautiful, requires effort of a moral kind. For Plato, only that rare art form which attracts the soul away from the ephemeral, the temporal, and toward the Absolute can be called great art.[59]

It is on essentially religious grounds, then, that Plato fears the artist, the copier of the phenomenal world. As Weil herself points out, Plato opposed contemporary artists because he believed they imitated only the transitory world (*NB*, 372). The artist, who always enjoys a certain prestige and who rarely possesses authentic religious or mystical knowledge, can lead his audiences away from the path of enlightenment by deceiving them with regard to what is ultimately real.[60] Plato's famous rejection of art[61]—a reluctant rejection, a reluctance inspired by a very real susceptibility to poetic charm—reflects an authentically spiritual attitude.

For Plato, a spiritual vision is won only with great difficulty. A process of education or conversion is necessary to turn the soul toward the supernatural. This painful process is required because the greater part of man is rooted in physical or natural reality. Despite his respect for the capacity of physical beauty to act as catalyst to spiritual growth,[62] Plato is skeptical regarding the spiritual value of beauty or charm in art. And yet, as that insightful twentieth-century Platonist, Iris Murdoch, has suggested, it can be said that in the *Timaeus*, the dialogue in which Plato attempts mythically to describe the creation of the world, Plato himself offers, if only implicitly, a positive model of artistic creativity.[63] As we shall see, Weil herself draws a theory of Platonic, Christian art from this particular dialogue.

Murdoch's claim concerning the artistic significance of Plato's *Timaeus* is a reasonable one, for, in all cultures past and present, cosmogonic myths provide the basis for any creative act,[64] including acts of artistic creativity. Indeed, from the point of view of the world religions, it is important that the artist model his work after that of the divine artificer. In this sense, perhaps, one may legitimately draw from Plato's description of the world's origin a positive theory of art to complement the negative view which we have based primarily on Plato's famous rejection of art in the *Republic*. As we will see, Weil follows Plato both in his negative assessment of the vast majority of artistic production and in his high regard (implicit, it is true, for Plato) for a certain rare and limited kind which models itself after the order of the world which was established by God at the time of creation.

This latter kind of art alone reveals rather than conceals ultimate or supernatural reality. Again, then, from a Platonic perspective, an artistic text must be evaluated in the light of values exterior and superior to it, values whose origins are supernatural.

Weil's own concept of the creation follows Plato's dialogue, the *Timaeus*, in important ways. Unlike Plato, however, and in accordance with the traditional Christian idea, Weil conceives of the creation as an act *ex nihilo* (from nothing). The *Timaeus* itself is a description of creation from chaos rather than *ex nihilo*. In this dialogue, therefore, the creator—the Demiurge or God—is not all-powerful, though he is all-good. In the *Timaeus*, the Demiurge, motivated by love of the Absolute Good, seeks to impose order on chaos or necessity, an irrational force indifferent to the good. In the act of creation, God persuades the brute force with which he is confronted toward the good, though he does so without changing the essential nature of necessity, which cannot be changed.[65] When necessity is persuaded toward the good, it is likewise persuaded toward the beautiful.[66] Also, neither the good (the divine) nor, therefore, the beautiful can be known except through knowledge of the necessary.[67]

This simple description of the creation of the world may then be viewed as a paradigm of artistic creativity. In keeping with the traditional concept of art as a reflection of the cosmic order,[68] good art, then, from a Platonic perspective, specifically, will reflect the order of the world as a double function of the necessary and the Good. Good art mirrors the natural and the supernatural, the former in a relationship of willing subordination to the latter. If, for Plato, the best art will reflect the order of the world in its totality and in its truth, then—taking his description of the creation of the world as an artistic paradigm—the subject matter of art includes not only physical nature but human nature as well. Both are works of the divine creation, a double function of the necessary and the Good from the origins of the world. The Good, however, will be revealed only through the necessary, although necessity is itself indifferent to the good. Inferior art, contrarily, will portray earthly existence without attention to the harsh facts of necessity or without an overriding vision of the Good. Rather than attending outward to things as they are, to the harsh conditions which define human existence—such conditions as mortality, suffering, and evil—the bad artist will build a world out of his own imaginings, wishes, or dreams and call it a picture of life. By failing to attend to the metallic hardness of necessity, a force to which every human being is subject against his hopes, he will never attain to knowledge of the deepest reality. The really real is not something cruel and natural—this describes necessity only—but, rather, supernatural and good. The profoundest reality is an absolute good toward which all things necessary tend.

Any kind of bad art, for Plato, will fail to do justice to, will fail to take properly and fairly into account, the objective, essentially harsh, order of things outside the self, that is, necessity itself. From an anachronistic perspective, this would include romantic and symbolist poetry, for example, when it offers (as it often, though not always, does offer) subjective or solipsistic ventures as discoveries of ultimate truth.[69]

Iris Murdoch helpfully uses the imagery Plato himself employs in the allegory of the cave to describe inadequate artistry as Plato might see it. These distinctions will help us to view modernist poetics, romantic and pragmatic, from a Platonic perspective.

Murdoch refers in the following passage to the prisoner chained in front of the fire who sees before him only the shadows of the objects passing behind and which he mistakes for the objects themselves, and also to the prisoner who has been freed and has turned to see the objects parading behind the fire, understanding the shadows now for the phantoms they actually are. Both of these cave dwellers, however, are completely unaware of ultimate reality, which exists outside the cave altogether: the realm of earth, sun, and water.

"The bad artist," Murdoch says, "...sees only moving shadows and construes the world in accordance with the easy unresisted mechanical causality of his personal dream life....The mediocre artist (the ironical man by the fire, if we may so characterize him), who thinks he 'knows himself but too well,' parades his mockery and spleen as a despairing dramatic rejection of any serious or just attempt to discern real order at all....Neither of these, as artist or as man, possesses...a just grasp of the hardness of the material which resists him, the necessity, the *anangke* of the world."[70] For Murdoch, in its way, each kind of art, the bad and the mediocre, is a lie about the way things are and therefore a stumbling block to man's knowledge about himself. Simply put, poor art ignores the central role of necessity in human life, the central import of suffering and evil. Inadequate art also fails to describe the existence of an absolute good (the world above the cave), a good which can be known only by means of the necessary.

Implicit already in this Platonic idea of bad and mediocre art we see a traditionalist critique of the modernist approaches to the interrelation of art and religion represented in this chapter by Nathan Scott and Giles Gunn. From the Platonic perspective, the romantic and pragmatic approaches to religious art falsify both art and religion by failing to seek ultimate meaning in the actual order of things. The romantic literary theorist, first, betrays reality. He does so by basing his view of art on physical Nature, to the exclusion of human nature. He thereby omits all serious consideration of the necessary, the hard facts of suffering and evil. Yet this is an art he calls religious in kind. His religion, omitting from view the problematic dimensions of human existence, is really nothing higher than the product of his own fantasy, a fulfillment of puerile wishes.

The pragmatic literary critic betrays the order of things by giving up as an impossibility the search for ultimate meaning at all. All attempts at an explanation of human existence are the product of fantasy. Individual societies, temporal realities, produce working fictions to help them endure. "Universal" problems such as suffering or evil are not contemplated. Yet, relativist premises do not stop the pragmatist from employing the word *religion.* Yet religion this modernist regards, simply, as one of the fictions with which societies strengthen themselves against adversity.

Plato's own view of religious art may be called authentic rather than sophistical. Platonic art is devoted to uncovering the ultimate truth about what is real. The truth, if courageously pursued to the limits of the necessary, will be discovered to contain a dimension which transcends empirical reality. If suffering and evil are encountered in their purity and in their truth, a sphere which transcends them both will be discovered: a realm both absolute and good. The Platonic literary critic, then, is symbolized by the courageous prisoner in the cave who painfully faces first the light of the fire and, subsequently, the blaze of the sun outside the cave.

Simone Weil not only describes but she offers an explanation for the existence of the romantic and the pragmatic approaches to the interrelation between literature and religion. Both views simultaneously assert a respect for religion and maintain premises actually antireligious. In a Platonic vein, Weil views inadequate artistry from an authentically religious perspective, one that affirms a natural and a supernatural realm mediated by a confrontation with necessity.

The outlooks we have termed "modernist" derive, Weil believes, from a desire to avoid the very problem which is the focal point of any good work of literature. The "romantic" and the "pragmatist" seek to escape an upsetting issue in terms of which all worldviews and, therefore, all theories of art, may in one way or another be explained. This disturbing problem constitutes a conflict between two contradictory forces, the existence of which the human being, in his uneducated or unconverted aspect, finds unbearable. The two opposing forces with which, according to Weil, every human being must in some way cope, and which he will do almost anything to escape facing, are good and evil.[71] According to Weil, the severely disturbing quality of the moral dimension of human existence causes many thinkers, at least in the modern period, simply to evade or deny its existence. This accounts for those who interpret life in the vein, respectively, of the romantic and the pragmatist we have examined. These thinkers regard human existence not as a moral phenomenon but rather as an aesthetic or a social reality—be this under religious or secular guise.

According to Weil, the aesthete hopes that by throwing a blanket of the beautiful over all actions and all things, by taking an attitude of openness toward all life has to offer, the problem of good and evil will never confront him. The aesthete may even, as the romantic literary critic does, offer up this attitude of relishing unconditionally all that exists as a religion, as a vision of ultimate reality, and as a guide to life. The man of purely social conscience belongs to a group where certain codes of behavior have been established and accepted by general agreement. He, too, then, believes himself excluded from any universal category of good and evil.[72] The purely social orientation, like the aesthetic, can take on a religious as well as a secular guise.[73]

Since the way of the beautiful and the way of the social cannot, of themselves, solve, but only evade, the problem of the opposition between good and evil, either approach to life—and, by implication, any approach to art based on these two attitudes—is doomed to failure. Weil suggests that the only alternative to the worship of beauty and the worship of state, though difficult, is at least possible. This final route, in fact, contains the means both to confront honestly and to resolve truthfully the opposition between good and evil. This alternative is the worship of God. Or, more broadly put, it is the way of the great religions, the way of mysticism. All of the religious traditions are grounded in mystical knowledge. Any religion, for Weil, which is not rooted in mysticism is a false religion. False religion, lacking a mystical ground, is unable either fully to face or to resolve the central—that is, the moral—problem of existence. For Simone Weil, mysticism ought to be the arbiter of all values, as all knowledge (*FLN*, 98). For Weil, as Christian and as mystic, the supreme Good in which the contraries good and evil are reconciled, the hidden and supreme mystery, likewise, of all great art, is the cross of Christ.

For Weil, a positive theory of art can not be separated from a vision of the cross, as Plato's cannot from a more general vision of an Absolute Good. The vast number of artists, however, produce only bad or mediocre art, because their inspiration is not supernatural. Most art is not true to life, because it fails to reflect the human condition in terms of good and evil in their essence. Bad art fails likewise to offer a means by which the apparent opposites, good and evil, may be reconciled. The instrument of this reconciliation is supernatural.

For Weil, the knowledge of a suprarational reality which great art requires only a genius of a religious kind can either grasp or reveal. On these grounds, Weil denounces the attitude concerning the artist which arose with romanticism. According to the romantic idea, the artist, simply by virtue of his emotional sensitivity and imaginative capacity, is endowed with peculiar "spiritual" powers which may legitimately guide the lives of nonartistic men and women. This attitude is consonant with the modern idea that religious and literary texts may be regarded as being on the same rather than on different levels of value: "What can and ought to be corrected...is the usurpation by writers of the function of spiritual guidance, for which they are totally unsuited.... Only writers of the highest order of genius in their full maturity are fit to exercise those functions. As for all other writers...their conception about life and the world and their opinions on current problems can have no interest at all, and it is absurd that they should be called upon to express them. This abuse dates from the 18th century, and especially from romanticism, and it has introduced into literature a Messianic afflatus wholly detrimental to its artistic purity" (*SNL*, 163).

Far from possessing a natural link to the spiritual, according to Weil, fiction tends to focus on phenomenal reality, making it suspect from a religious perspective. Art tends by nature to offer as ultimate what is only apparent reality. Only an artistic genius of the highest order can impart a vision of the really real, that is, a picture of human existence as a function of good and evil in their truth, as opposites reconciled in a higher Good which is absolute. Weil allows for a certain—rare—kind of art which is not detrimental to the auditor or reader in a spiritual sense because it reveals rather than conceals ultimate reality.

Weil bases her positive view of art on Plato's vision of a natural and a supernatural realm which find a mediating principle. For this reason, her poetics may be called sacramental in a genuine rather than in a spurious or sophistical sense. Weil's idea of the world's origin will furnish a starting point for an analysis of her positive view of art. Already in this crucial respect, the cross of Christ plays a central role.[74] Thus, religious mystery, and not philosophy or anthropology, undergirds her approach to the interrelation between art and religion.

Weil shares the metaphysical vision contained in Plato's *Timaeus*. She adopts Plato's vision of two realms, a natural (necessity) and a supernatural (the Good), which require and find mediation. This limited dualism—as distinct from radical or Manichaean dualism, where the two distinct realms neither seek nor find a point of unity—provides the basis for the mystical outlook in all religious traditions.[75] Weil suggests that any work of art worthy of the name ought to imitate the order of the world the *Timaeus* describes. In her notebooks Weil writes, "Plato—*Timaeus*. He gives a double explanation of the world, first as the result of a divine cause, secondly as the result of a necessary cause....Art is an imitation of this" (*NB*, 98). Weil takes also from the *Timaeus* the idea that the divine can be known only through the necessary (*NB*, 25, 26, 65–66).

Whereas for Plato the Demiurge acts as mediator between chaos or the necessary, and the Good; for Weil it is the Logos, the Christ—and him crucified—who fulfills this function. Where Plato describes a creation from chaos, Weil describes the creation in traditional Christian fashion, that is, *ex nihilo*. But rather than the usual idea of *ex nihilo*, which emphasizes God's power, Weil's idea of creation from nothing connotes a void which God makes within himself in a voluntary act of self-emptying or withdrawal.[76] From this void, this nothing, created in an act of self-giving love or self-loss, something other than God is born. Thus, self-emptying, and not self-assertion, becomes the fundamental creative principle. Weil interprets the Genesis story of Adam and Eve in light of this essentially tragic conception.[77]

God, though all-powerful, lovingly renounces his power when he creates the world. In an act of love, he surrenders himself to necessity. Necessity constitutes all which imposes itself upon the human being against his will. Necessity is a force which is foreign to the divine nature, because, unlike God, who is all-good, necessity is indifferent to the good. God empties himself in this way in order that the human being might return God's love with a perfect love of his own. By accepting necessity, the source of affliction, man may realize a God-like love. This very act of acceptance itself constitutes a form of love which is self-emptying to the point of perfection. The Father's self-emptying act of creation occurs through the agency of Christ crucified.

Whenever love triumphs in a state of extreme accursedness (affliction), the human soul shares in the love of the crucified Christ for the Father at the moment of abandonment. In this mysterious self-sacrificial love the world itself originates. The world is so made that all creatures, no less than the crucified one, are able to love God with perfect purity, perfect selflessness (*NB*, 279, 344). It is in this capacity of the natural world to make possible a mutual self-emptying love between man and God that its goodness as well as its beauty lies. Great art will articulate a call to contemplate the cruciform beauty of the world.

The romantic would imbue the poetry of the West with a spiritual vision which contains no reference to the religious mysteries of the Judeo-Christian tradition.[78] Contrarily, for Weil, the crucified Christ's cry of abandonment sounds through every word of great poetry (*L*, 103). Any truly spiritual work of art will, in some way, evoke the crucified God. The salient characteristic of such a work is a combined tone of bitterness, on the one hand, and, on the other, tenderness. The bitterness recalls the despairing cry of a person who is crushed by the blind fate or necessity which has regulated human life since the world's origins. The serenity evokes a person who, in an act of perfect or divine love, maintains an attitude of patience or gentleness even in the depths of humiliation and despair (*IC*, 48). The combination of bitterness and serenity is the only source of pure beauty in art, because it alone evokes the perfect, redeeming love of the divine criminal. It alone evokes the cross of Christ, the mysterious supernatural source of the reconciliation between good and evil. In the cross, the natural contraries which cause the wretchedness of human existence are dissolved. Thus, by imitating the cross, tragic art may be said to strike a harmonious chord which sounds in every corner of the world.

The secret of great art, then, for Weil, is that in it the impossible is accomplished; that is, in it one essential and unrecognized truth is revealed: "Everything that is good is of divine and supernatural origin, and proceeds directly or indirectly from the celestial, transcendental source of all good. Everything that proceeds from another source, everything whose origin is natural, is alien to the good" (*FLN*, 120). Thus, Weil proposes an idea of good and evil which transcends the didacticism with which romantics commonly identify and consequently eschew the moral concern of literature.[79]

The great artist understands that virtually everything in this world is subject to the rule of chance. This painful awareness makes it possible for him to reveal the supernatural quality of the good, the love without condition which mysteriously and secretly undergirds the world's order—the cross of Christ. It is precisely the conditional nature of the finite which pantheism and, with it, romanticism either overlooks or denies.[80] For the Hindu, as for the Buddhist, ascribing absolute value to the relative, as the philosophical monist does, is the source of all ignorance.[81] This proclivity is, likewise, the principle of idolatry which it is the particular goal of the Protestant Christian to abolish.[82] It is only when the natural world is perceived in its truth, as a force indifferent to the good, that the empirical realm ceases to be worshiped. Only then does the sacred dimension of the human soul come to light: the human being's capacity to love God perfectly. In tragic phrase, without a courageous facing of the outer defeat to which every human being is subject, man's deepest and truest victory, an inner triumph, can never be realized.

As the spiritual genius, St. Francis of Assisi, sought poverty not for the sake of sorrow but for the sake of truth and beauty (*TME*, 14), so the great poet gravitates toward the tragic in order to unveil the essential beauty or goodness of the world. Certain high tragedies—of Aeschylus, Sophocles, Shakespeare, and Racine—offer the order of things in all its true frightfulness. Concomitantly, these dramas reveal a mysterious beneficence which is absolute.

The following chapter will argue that only an understanding of Christianity in its esoteric or mystical dimension, only a viewing of the Christian faith from the perspective of *theologia crucis* (theology of the cross), can truly reveal the affinity that exists between the Christian and the tragic visions. Weil's insights into the mystery of the cross, particularly as the cross relates to the act of divine creation, will provide a mystical or esoteric theory of Christian tragedy. This theory may act as guide to a longstanding debate which places in doubt the possibility of harmonizing a Christian with a tragic worldview.

Notes

1. For an in-depth discussion of the word *tradition* in its spiritual meaning, see "What Is Tradition?", ch. 2 of Nasr, *Knowledge and the Sacred*.

2. Simone Weil is the unique example of speculative mystical Christian Platonism in our century. On this point, see Miklos Vetö, "The Ethics of Simone Weil" (1964), p. 427.

3. All religious traditions place great importance on the analogy of human and divine artificer. See, e.g., Ananda K.

Coomaraswamy, *Christian and Oriental Philosophy of Art* (1956), p. 73.

4. For a lucid study of Heidegger's view of the divine as it relates to poetry, see James L. Perotti, *Heidegger on the Divine: The Thinker, the Poet and God* (1974). The many works of Nathan Scott illustrate the modern romantic idea of literature as the reflection of a secular or natural sacrality, and the influence of Heidegger features prominently in Scott's later work. For single studies espousing a kindred sense of natural or secular sacrality, see, e.g., Eugene Webb, *The Dark Dove: The Sacred and the Secular in Modern Literature* (1975); John Killinger, *The Fragile Presence: Transcendence in Modern Literature* (1973).

5. The work of Giles Gunn well illustrates the anthropological or cultural approach to the study of literature and religion. An indication of the wide influence of this approach to the study of religion and literature may be obtained by reading David Hesla, "Religion and Literature: The Second Stage," *Journal of the American Academy of Religion*, vol. 46, no. 2, pp. 181–92.

6. For an explanation of the Sufi term "eye of the heart," see ch. 4, "Scientia Sacra" in Nasr, *Knowledge and the Sacred*, esp. pp. 148–52. For a discussion of faith as the mystical mode of knowledge in Christianity, see ch. 8, "Universality and Particular Nature of the Christian Tradition" in Frithjof Schuon, *The Transcendent Unity of Religions* (1953), esp. pp. 156–63.

7. Each of the following standard studies of religion confirms the fact that, according to the religious traditions, *ultimate* reality has a supernatural or sacred or invisible quality as opposed to a natural or profane or visible character. See, e.g. Smith, *Religions of Man*, pp. 462–63; Eliade, *Sacred and the Profane*, pp. 11, 118, 202; Otto, *Idea of the Holy*, pp. xvi–xix, 11, 163; Ninian Smart, *The Religious Experience of Mankind* (1986), p. 15.

8. One can detect a clear decline in the association of the study of literature and religion with the Christian

tradition, for example, in the four stages of the discipline's history outlined by Giles Gunn in *The Interpretation of Otherness: Literature, Religion, and the American Imagination* (1979), pp. 19–51. This secularization appears to have triumphed by the time of David Hesla's article. (See n. 5, above.) This tendency has been noted in passing in recent British scholarship, as, for example in David Jasper, *The Study of Literature and Religion: An Introduction* (1989), pp. 1–2; and in T. R. Wright, *Theology and Literature* (1988), p. 8. To my knowledge, however, traditionalists and modernists have nowhere engaged in debate concerning the fundamental issues at stake in this important interdisciplinary field.

9. Underhill, *Mysticism*, p. 43.

10. For a study of Platonic mediation in the thought of Simone Weil, see Springsted, *Christus Mediator.*

11. The following may be classified as classic studies of the relationship between art and religion from the perspective of one or more religious traditions: Hans Urs Von Balthasar, *The Glory of the Lord: A Theological Aesthetics* (1982–c. 1989); Henri Brémond, *Prière et poésie* (1926); Coomaraswamy, *Christian and Oriental Philosophy of Art*; T. S. Eliot, "Religion and Literature," in *Selected Essays* (1946), pp. 92–115; Jacques Maritain, *Creative Intuition in Art and Poetry* (1953); Gerardus Van Der Leeuw, *Sacred and Profane Beauty: The Holy in Art* (1963).

12. On the subject of the rightful subordination of art to spiritual knowledge, see Ray Livingston, *The Traditional Theory of Literature* (1962), pp. 101, 117, 126; Coomaraswamy, *Christian and Oriental Philosophy of Art*, pp. 96, 107–8; Schuon, *Transcendent Unity of Religions*, p. 96.

13. The works of Nathan Scott include "The Modern Experiment in Criticism: A Theological Approach," in *The New Orpheus: Essays toward a Christian Poetic* (1964), pp. 141–171; *The Broken Center: Studies in the Theological Horizon of Modern Literature* (1966); *Negative Capability: Studies in the New Literature and the Religious Situation*

(1969); *The Wild Prayer of Longing: Poetry and the Sacred* (1971); *The Poetics of Belief* (1985).

14. Nathan Scott was one of the pioneers in the study of the interrelation between literature and religion in the United States. Early in Scott's career, in the 1960s, Scott proposed the religious approach to literature as an alternative to the critical orientation popular at that time, commonly known as the New Criticism. The group of scholars who called themselves the New Critics sought to seal a poetic text off from the circumambient world, regarding its language—a rich, connotative language unavailable to the scientist—rather than its subject matter as being of chief interest and importance. Scott suggests, in opposition to the New Critics, that it is not the language, the medium, but rather the content, the vision of the poet, that controls a work of art. Scott proceeds to claim that insofar as every literary text reflects a poet's vision, it may be said to be religious. Scott draws on the liberal theology of Paul Tillich in order to support this contention. Tillich himself defines religion not in the manner in which the religious traditions do but, more generally, in philosophical terms. For Tillich, a person's religion is his ultimate concern. Scott claims, thus, that the religious ground of any cultural creation is the ultimate concern to which it gives expression. Thus, in a fashion typical of the modernist, already in this early period, Scott acknowledges no perceptible boundary between the two domains of literature and religion: "The religious dimension is something intrinsic to and constitutive of the nature of literature as such" ("The Modern Experiment in Criticism," p. 160).

15. Scott, *Poetics of Belief*, p. 13.

16. It is interesting to note that both Wallace Stevens's idea of decreation, mentioned in the previous paragraph, and Heidegger's concept of *Gelassenheit* (letting be), in the present paragraph, are Weilian concepts. Whereas Weil insists upon the ethical content of each process, Stevens and Heidegger omit it. The outlook of the latter thinkers

necessitates this omission, for it regards physical nature or the world of things, rather than human nature or the inner world of man, as the locus of the holy. The presence or absence of ethical content, respectively, may be said to distinguish a romantic or magical from a traditional or genuinely religious view of sacred activity.

17. Smart, e.g., includes the ethical aspect as one of the five fundamental dimensions of religion (*Religious Experience of Mankind*, p. 9). For Otto, in a similar vein, the sacred or the holy is constituted by two essential elements—the irrational or numinous and the rational or ethical. See, especially, ch. 13, "The Two Processes of Development," in *Idea of the Holy*.

18. Irving Babbitt has been the most trenchant critic of the romantic tendency to substitute what is essentially pantheistic revery for costly spiritual effort, without relinquishing the tones of consecration suitable to authentic religion alone. (See, e.g., ch. 8, "Romantic Irony," in *Rousseau and Romanticism* (1919), esp. pp. 285–90.)

19. For an incisive critique of the general modernist tendency to view life in aesthetic terms, see ch. 6, "Life, Art, and Peace," in Joseph Wood Krutch's *The Modern Temper: A Study and a Confession* (1929). Although, as a modernist himself, Krutch regards traditional religion as a thing of the past, yet, unlike the romantic modernist, he recognizes that aesthetics can itself provide no substitute for traditional religion, because it provides no ethical dimension and therefore no satisfactory guide to life.

20. Father William Lynch's widely quoted study of literature and religion, *Christ and Apollo: The Dimensions of the Literary Imagination* (1960), offers a helpful distinction between what he calls the "univocal" and the "analogical" imagination. The former—as, for example, the aesthetic (or the didactic) imagination—tends to suppress rather than to acknowledge the contraries at work in the world, good and evil. By contrast, the analogical or genuinely ethical imagi-

nation gives fair attention both to the facts of good and evil and to the distinctions that exist between them. According to Lynch, the univocal mind, unlike the analogical, is uninvolved, uncommitted, imposing its own view of things on the world rather than humbly observing it, learning from it, describing it as it is (pp. 124–25).

21. Maritain speaks of Romanticism as "pseudo-prophetic revelation, bound up with magic and the search for transmuting reality through the power of words" (*Creative Intuition*, p. 194). He indicates further that magic has a special appeal in the modern world because of the predominant influence of rationalism (p. 233). According to Maritain, the poet escapes the temptation to magic only if he is willing to renounce the will to power (ibid., pp. 232–33). For Maritain, as for any traditionalist, poetry is an essentially disinterested activity. Maritain's linking magic with the will to power coincides with Underhill's distinction between mysticism and magic. The former, she asserts, is a process of self-naughting or self-emptying. The latter is a form of self-seeking, only putatively a concern for ultimate things (*Mysticism*, pp. 71, 164).

Like romanticism, symbolism also suffers from the tendency to mistake the magical for the real. Marcel Raymond speaks of the propensity of poetry from the nineteenth century onward to offer itself as a substitute for religion, becoming an instrument of irregular metaphysical knowledge (*From Baudelaire to Surrealism* (1961), p. 5). The traditionalist must agree with Maritain that any artist who attempts to produce art which contains an ultimate or supernatural significance—outside the context of any religious tradition—suffers from a profound illusion. Maritain refers, for example, to the creation of entire myth systems by such modern poets as W. B. Yeats or Ezra Pound as woefully self-contradictory. Any myth which authentically imbues a work of art must be believed in by the whole man, perceived as true in a universal sense and not be created by the man himself for the sake of his art (*Creative Intuition*, p. 181).

22. On the fusion of morality and religion with aesthetics in the tragedy of Aeschylus and Sophocles, see "The Drama of Aeschylus" and "Sophocles and the Tragic Character" in Werner Jaeger's *Archaic Greece/The Mind of Athens* (1965). On this subject see also William Chase Greene, *Moira: Fate, Good, and Evil in Greek Thought* (1944). Similarly, the moral emphasis of Shakespeare's plays, as well as those of Aeschylus and Sophocles, is well illustrated in Lewis Campbell's *Tragic Drama in Aeschylus, Sophocles, and Shakespeare* (1904).

23. Giles Gunn's most important ideas on the subject of literature and religion may be found in *Interpretation of Otherness.*

24. H. S. Thayer, "Pragmatism," in *Encyclopedia of Philosophy* (1972), pp. 430–35.

25. *The Culture of Criticism and the Criticism of Culture* (1987), p. 64.

26. Gunn, *Culture of Criticism*, p. 180.

27. The similarities between the ancient sophist's outlook on life and art and those of Gunn, the modern pragmatist, are astonishing. See Rupert Lodge, *Plato's Theory of Art* (1953), esp. pp. 20, 37, 68. Indeed, Lodge explicitly contrasts Plato, opponent of the sophists, with the American pragmatist, John Dewey (pp. 252–54).

28. Gunn, *Interpretation of Otherness*, p. 96.

29. Ibid., pp. 95–96.

30. Ibid., pp. 35–6.

31. William James Earle, "William James," in *Encyclopedia of Philosophy* (1972), p. 244.

32. Gunn, *Interpretation of Otherness*, pp. 111–12.

33. From a traditional perspective, on the contrary, either religious myth is true now or it was never true at all. See Livingston, *Traditional Theory of Literature*, p. 67.

34. From Heidegger's "Hölderlin and the Essence of Poetry," quoted in Perotti, *Heidegger on the Divine*, p. 104.

35. Gunn, *Interpretation of Otherness*, p. 113.

36. Ibid., p. 178.

37. Ibid., p. 188.

38. Ibid.

39. Nasr, *Knowledge and the Sacred*, p. 3.

40. Ray Livingston discusses the two-self psychology as it applies to literature in *The Traditional Theory of Literature*, a study of literature from the perspective of the traditionalist art critic Ananda Coomaraswamy. See esp. pp. 17–22. Also of interest is Livingston's discussion of Coomaraswamy's idea of catharsis (p. 100). See, further, Henri Brémond's assertion that Aristotle empties the term "catharsis" of its original, mystical content (*Prière et Poésie*, pp. 194–95).

From a strictly religious point of view, Mircea Eliade suggests the importance of the two-self psychology, the death and rebirth of the soul, in the religions of both archaic and highly evolved societies in ch. 4, "Human Existence and Sanctified Life," of *The Sacred and the Profane*.

41. Nasr, *Knowledge and the Sacred*, pp. 137–38.

42. Gunn betrays a misunderstanding of traditional religion not only when he ignores the two-self psychology which the religious traditions propose but also by his use of general terms. Gunn does not set as the goal of his project to offer poetry as a substitute for religion, as Scott does; yet his very discussion of what he continues to call 'religious' experience in a post-Christian age betrays a way of looking at the world which differs thoroughly from the religious experience of the traditions. From a traditional perspective, therefore, another word ought to be used.

As an example of his sophistical use of language, Gunn uses the word *transcendent* to describe profane or natural rather than sacred or supernatural reality (the latter word in each pair constitutes the original, traditional referent for the term). For example, Gunn offers Jay Gatsby's obsession with Daisy Buchanan in F. Scott Fitzgerald's *Great Gatsby* as a form of transcendence, as a dimension of religious experience, in a post-Christian age. After doing so, Gunn speaks generally of what he takes the "transcendent" to be: "Without the tug of the transcendent life would be colorless and monotonous, lacking in radiance" (*Interpretation of Otherness*, p. 221). Gunn uses the term 'religious' at the outset of the book, in a manner similar to his use of 'transcendent' above: "Experience needs no transempirical justification in order to be understood religiously; experience itself is more wonderful than any philosophy or theology" (ibid., p. 8).

As for Scott, for Gunn also, then, it is the wonderfulness of reality, its color and radiance, that is offered up as its religious or transcendent dimension. Thus, as is to be expected, the romantic and the pragmatic empiricist meet in the realm of the senses, their common ground. For reasons it would be interesting to explore, each obfuscates as well as he can his own empiricist premises by couching his scientistic outlook in religious language.

43. Nasr, *Knowledge and the Sacred*, p. 253.

44. See Livingston, *Traditional Theory of Literature.*

45. Scott, *Wild Prayer of Longing*, p. 73.

46. Scott, *Poetics of Belief*, pp. 66–67.

47. Scott, *Wild Prayer of Longing*, pp. 48–49, 51.

48. According to the Gospel of John, which is the most mystical of the four gospels (L. William Countryman, *The Mystical Way in the Fourth Gospel* (1987)), the eucharist is a re-presentation of the crucifixion itself rather than a commemoration of the Last Supper, as in the Synoptics. On this point, see John Marsh (ed.), *The Gospel of John*, in *The Pelican New Testament Commentaries* (1983), p. 56.

49. Feuerbach quoted in Walter Kasper, *The God of Jesus Christ* (1984), p. 29.

50. Monika K. Hellwig, "Sacrament: Christian Sacraments," in *Encyclopedia of Religion* (1987), vol. 12, p. 504.

51. Hellwig, "Sacrament," p. 506.

52. Smith, *Religions of Man*, pp. 462–63.

53. According to Nasr, certain Muslims have regarded Plato as a prophet (*Knowledge and the Sacred*, p. 35); Socrates, similarly, has been viewed in certain early Christian circles as a pre-Christian saint (ibid., p. 61, n. 114). Nasr himself believes that a rediscovery of the sacred character of knowledge in our time would result in a reappraisal of Plato and other ancients as possessors of eternal or sacred knowledge (ibid., p. 35).

54. Ibid., p. 34.

55. See Nasr, for example, on the implications of the revival of Platonism in early nineteenth-century England and in the poetry of William Blake (ibid., pp. 97–99).

56. On this point, see Otto, *Idea of the Holy*, pp. 94–95.

57. My treatment of Plato's view of art has been influenced throughout by Iris Murdoch's *The Fire and the Sun: Why Plato Banished the Artists* (1977).

58. Plato, *Republic, in The Collected Dialogues of Plato* (1961), book VII, pp. 747–72.

59. The religious traditions generally regard the character of Ultimate Reality as both absolute and good (Nasr, *Knowledge and the Sacred*, pp. 134–35).

60. It is precisely this same fear which, in his own day, T. S. Eliot expresses in his important essay, "Religion and Literature." Note, for example, the following passage: "What I do wish to affirm is that the whole of modern literature is corrupted by what I call secularism, that it is simply unaware of, simply cannot understand the meaning of, the primacy of the supernatural over the natural life: of something which I assume to be our primary concern" (p. 110).

61. Plato, *Republic*, book X, pp. 819–33. (See also book III, pp. 630–43.)

62. See, e.g., Plato's *Phaedrus* and *Symposium*.

63. Murdoch, *Fire and the Sun*, p. 49.

64. Charles H. Long, "Cosmogony," in *Encyclopedia of Religion* (1987), vol. 4, p. 94.

65. Plato, *The Timaeus*, in *The Collected Dialogues of Plato* (1961), p. 1175.

66. Ibid., p. 1162.

67. Ibid., p. 1192.

68. Livingston, *Traditional Theory of Literature*, p. 31.

69. See n. 21, above, for a discussion of the tendency of the romantic, as the symbolist, to mistake magical incantation for religious truth. This tendency, it would seem, only the lyric—as opposed to the epic or the tragic—poet is apt to fall into. The latter kinds of poets take as their subject, perforce, the relationship between the individual and the exterior world. Necessarily, therefore, they avoid any urge to offer private feelings and imaginings as descriptions of what is ultimately real. It is true, however, that not every romantic or symbolist poet professes prophetic powers. For example, although among the romantic poets, Wordsworth and Coleridge do assume a prophetic pose (at least in their early work), John Keats and Emily Dickinson do not. So among symbolist poets, whereas Stéphane Mallarmé and Arthur Rimbaud assume a vatic stance, Anna Akhmatova and T. S. Eliot do not. In this regard, A. S. P. Woodhouse offers a useful discussion of the relationship between the major English poets and the Christian tradition in *The Poet and His Faith: Religion and Poetry in England from Spenser to Eliot and Auden* (1965).

70. Murdoch, *Fire and the Sun*, p. 76.

71. The following discussion rests on the ideas contained in Weil's late essay, "Cette guerre est une guerre

de religions," in *Écrits de Londres et dernières lettres* (1957), pp. 98–108.

72. The idea of a strictly social conscience reveals its destructive potential most clearly in the "revolutionary conscience" of V. I. Lenin and in the "higher law of the party" of Adolf Hitler (see, e.g., Paul Johnson, *Modern Times: The World from the 20s to the 80s* (1983), pp. 85–86, 181). Both leaders believed that acts of violence performed in the name of a political or cultural ideology are permissible in a moral sense.

73. Note, e.g., that "*Gott mit uns*" (God with us) was the slogan worn on the belts of Nazi soldiers (Charles McCarthy, "Meditations on August 9, Our Day of Affliction: O Emmanuel!", in *The Other Side* (1990), p. 12). Similarly, the mass killings of the sixteenth-century Spanish Inquisition were putatively perpetrated in the name of God, though actually on behalf of the church as a social institution.

74. Another Christian author, Gerardus Van der Leeuw, like Weil, approaches artistic creations, as the creation of the world, from the perspective of the redemption. For Van der Leeuw, as for Weil, the entire theological aesthetic is contained in the image of the crucified. See pt. 7, "Theological Aesthetics," of Van der Leeuw, *Sacred and Profane Beauty*, esp. pp. 327–30.

75. Underhill, *Mysticism*, p. 43.

76. For Weil, St. John's description of the Lamb slain from the foundation of the world means God emptied himself in the act of creation (*WG*, 145). Weil calls attention also to Paul's statement that God created the world through Christ (*FLN*, 239).

For a discussion of the biblical basis for the ideas both of the preexistence of the crucified Jesus and of the creation as an act which occurs through the agency of Christ, see Walter Kasper (*God of Jesus Christ*, pp. 174–77); Jürgen Moltmann (*God in Creation* (1991), p. 94). An assessment of Weil's own contribution to the concept of the creation as it relates to the kenosis or self-emptying of God, an act that culminates in the cross (see Paul's Letter to the Philippians 2:5–11 for the *locus classicus* of the kenotic motif), may be found in Geddes MacGregor, *He Who Let Us Be: A Theology of Love* (1975), pp. 56–57, 73–75, 120–22, 185.

77. "Adam and Eve sought for divinity in vital energy—in a tree, a fruit," says Weil. "But it is prepared for us on some dead wood, geometrically squared, upon which hangs a corpse. We must look for the secret of our kinship with God in our mortality" (*NB*, 235). Thus, by eating the fruit, Adam and Eve sought to be like God through an act of self-affirmation. Their deed indicates that they longed for divinity without understanding it. For Weil, again, as for Plato, the divine can be known or experienced only through the necessary. Because they were ignorant of God's own nature, Adam and Eve did not apprehend that the true path to being like God is the path of renunciation. The vocation of the human being is, in fact, to be like God; but God, before he is anything else, is love; and love, before it is anything else, is pure or sacrificial. The suffering to which Adam and Eve become subject as a result of an original act of disobedience, therefore, is not something punitive; rather, it is God's greatest gift; it is an invitation actually to become like him by loving perfectly.

"Man has sinned in trying to become God (on the imaginary plane)," says Weil, "and God has redeemed this sin by becoming man. By which means man can really become *sicut deus*. Thus the serpent had spoken truly" (*NB*, 235). For Weil, then, by way of the cross, Christ offers both a model and a means for responding to the perfect self-emptying love of the creator even as Jesus did in the moment of loving dereliction on the cross, a perfect love possible only in affliction. Affliction itself is a condition available to man only after the fall, when human beings have left paradise. In tragic phrase, only in affliction, then, a torment which constitutes the greatest possible outer defeat, is the human being's deepest inner victory—perfect Christlike love—made possible. This love constitutes the assimilation to the divine for which Adam and Eve originally longed without knowing.

78. It is interesting to trace in the study of A. S. P. Woodhouse a gradual decline in the themes of repentance and redemption, as one approaches and enters the Romantic period, i.e., after Milton and through Shelley (*The Poet and His Faith*).

79. For a classic example of the romantic's equating the moral purport of literature with a didactic intent, see Edgar Allan Poe, "The Poetic Principle," in *Criticism: The Major Texts* (1970), pp. 352–57. As an example of this tendency in contemporary romantic criticism, Bernard Bosanquet regards as "dependent" rather than "free" any beauty which is placed in the service of a moral ideal (*A History of Aesthetic* (1910), p. 272). From a traditionalist's perspective, Irving Babbitt denounces helpfully the romantic reduction of the moral to the didactic and, with it, the consequent attestation that art should exist for its own sake (*Rousseau and Romanticism*, p. 204).

80. Schuon, *Transcendent Unity of Religions*, pp. 55–56.

81. Nasr, *Knowledge and the Sacred*, p. 292.

82. Smith, *Religions of Man*, p. 469.

Chapter Two

Simone Weil and Christian Tragedy

Two ideas in particular mark Weil's theory of tragedy, like her broader conception of spiritual art, as sacramental. Weil's mystical understanding of catharsis (purification) and her esoteric conception of divine justice challenge modern skeptical and rationalist Christian views of tragic catharsis and tragic theodicy. In contradiction of opposing views, Weil believes that tragedy mediates a supernatural reality.

According to Simone Weil, it is the mysterious or hidden capacity of the created world to enable man to return the folly of love of God's original creative act—and not, for example, the universe's rational distribution of reward and punishment—which may be said to render its author just. This is a kind of divine justice which only a tragic world, one harsh but purposeful, may reveal. Comcomitantly, it is the creation of the world itself, an act of perfect self-emptying love on the part of God, an act of the Father realized through the cross of Christ, that enables the human being to achieve spiritual perfection. A divine dimension may be awakened within the human soul through a painful catharsis or purification of the whole being. This state of perfection occurs whenever an afflicted soul acquiesces to her destiny in a spirit of gentle love. Thus, Weil's concepts of divine justice and tragic catharsis both spring from her mystical conception of the world's creation, an act of the Father mediated through Christ's cross.

As we have seen in the previous chapter, Weil describes the divine creation as an act of perfect self-giving love. Thus, when he creates the world, God, though all-powerful, renounces his power. At the origin of the world, God surrenders himself to necessity, a force indifferent to the good and therefore foreign to his own nature. By creating the world as a force blind to the good, God, himself all-good, enables man to return God's perfect act of self-giving with a perfect, self-emptying act of his own. The human being's responsive love is perfect when it, too, is utterly self-renouncing. The person's acquiescence to necessity, a consent made perfect when a love for the good triumphs in affliction, constitutes the mediating agency between the human and the divine. This is a harmonizing moment, a moment of perfect love in which every human being seeking perfection is invited to share. The supreme spiritual victory comprises participation in the abandoned Christ's perfect trust in the Father: This love rises out of a wretchedness which shatters the heart. Thus, in tragic terms, the order of the world, its harshness, enables spiritual purification or catharsis of soul. The universe's invitation to spiritual perfection through participation in Christ's cross, then, and not its guarantee of fair punishments and rewards, reveals the hand of a just God.

Weil's concept of catharsis, set within the framework of her cosmogony, helps to return the concept of tragic purification to an original mystical sense. A Weilian idea of catharsis implicitly evokes Plato, the Orphics, the Pythagoreans, the initiates at Eleusis, all of whom employed the word *catharsis* in a spiritual way before Aristotle emptied it of mystical content.[1]

For Simone Weil, as mystical Christian Platonist, the locus of catharsis, purification, or tragic resolution is neither the pure reason nor the practical reason of the philosophers but rather the mystic's *fundus animae*, the *Seelengrund*, the Intellect, the faculty through which sacred knowledge may be attained.[2] Mystical knowledge is a gnosis which only a painful experience of the entire being can yield. Reason alone cannot uncover it.

From the perspective of the religious traditions, great art must always contain an element of shock, the metallic hardness of facts which impose themselves upon human beings against their will. Trauma is needed to awaken the soul from its slumber (a natural state), that is, to humiliate the ego and thereby purify the inner self so that the soul's latent potential to apprehend the really real, the supernatural, may become actualized. For the traditionalist, great art is itself a potential means of catharsis or spiritual purification.[3]

Weil shares the traditionalist view that art may have a cathartic or purifying effect. What distinguishes Weil's idea of purification from that of other traditionalists is her belief that the supernatural good which is revealed by a process of shattering purgation is the perfect, self-emptying love of the Christ for the Father at the moment of forsakenness. This good only an art tragic in kind may reveal. Thus, Weil's traditionalist poetics is specifically Christian and, as we shall see, characteristically tragic, at the same time.

Because her concept of tragedy is rooted in religious mystery, Simone Weil proffers an idea of tragic catharsis markedly different from the concepts formulated by the most influential theorists of tragedy. Weil's view of catharsis differs from the strictly philosophical notions of thinkers such as Aristotle, Hegel, or Nietzsche. Aristotle, like Weil, values tragedy as a source of knowledge, a knowledge universal in kind.[4] Aristotle, however, suggests that tragedy reveals knowledge of the empirical sphere alone. The value of tragedy, from an Aristotelian perspective, lies in its imitation of action, an action entirely human.[5] This action is terrible and pitiful. Through its presentation, one may, through the purgation of painful emotion (catharsis), gain insight into the universal laws that govern human behavior. The locus of tragic resolution, or catharsis, a resolution the arousing of disturbing emotions requires, is reason. Reason is the source of tragic insight concerning human behavior in its universal or probable aspect. By means of tragic experience, reason becomes purged or purified of disturbing emotions, the mind left to reap the harvest of rational insight.[6] Thus, not the *fundus animae*, as from a Weilian perspective, but reason serves as the locus of tragic resolution for Aristotle.

Ostensibly, the source of tragic catharsis, for Hegel, is an absolute or eternal rather than a finite reality. Yet, upon examination, the actual source of tragic resolution revealed in Hegel's work is history. Hegel himself, however, contends that the tragic poet attains to knowledge of a sacred character. For Hegel, the poet perceives the work of the transcendent (Absolute Spirit), where others perceive only the chaos of nature; the tragedian sees in finite conflicts an infinite significance, because he perceives the resolution of these conflicts as something necessary; the tragic poet sees Eternal Justice vindicated where others see only the senseless fate of finite individuals.[7] But despite Hegel's religious use of language and in spite of his equating at times the Absolute Spirit of his philosophical system with the Divine Providence of Christianity,[8] for Hegel, there is, in tragedy, as in history, no pointing upward to a reality which transcends the natural order. Hegel identifies Being with becoming, the historical sphere. This fact obviates the possibility of the human being's actuating the deepest ground of the soul, the *fundus animae* or *Seelengrund*, as it is actuated only in religious experience. Spiritual Self-actualization presupposes the existence of a realm transcendent to the human being (though accessible to him through pain). Hegel, then, maintains that the dramatic poet reveals essential or explicit truth about the divine order. Hegel, however, does not share the dualistic outlook of the religious traditions. One may thus say that Hegel uses, as the romantic literary critic also tends to use, religious language sophistically. Though Hegel's Absolute Spirit is transcendent in the sense that it is not to be identified with any particular finite thing or things, yet it is not transcendent as the creator of the world is transcendent.[9]

Unlike Aristotle and Hegel, Nietzsche regards art, including tragic art, not as a means of revealing but rather as a way of transmuting or conquering reality.[10] Rather than being a means to attaining universal knowledge of a rational kind, tragedy becomes the means to achieving private redemption. The substance of this "redemption" is aesthetic. Life can be justified only in terms of a beauty which is separated from the good; it can be justified only in aesthetic and not in moral or certainly supramoral terms.[11] For Nietzsche, this means life may be justified only through art and, for him, supremely, tragedy.[12] Thus, by claiming religious effects for something he actually views in aesthetic terms, Nietzsche offers, even more clearly than Hegel does, an example of the tendency of the romantic modernist to ascribe a magical quality to art and concomitantly to employ religious language sophistically. For Nietzsche, the locus of resolution to the tragic perception of a chaotic world order is neither the reason of the spectator, as for Aristotle, nor the rational order of history, as for Hegel, but rather the illusion of art. Nietzsche, then, in the vein of the critics lauded by Nathan Scott in chapter 1, in this sense offers tragic poetry as a substitute for religion. From a traditional perspective, he speaks of the irrational or subrational (the sensual) in terms which ought legitimately to be reserved for the suprarational.

Unlike Aristotle, Hegel, and Nietzsche, then, Weil regards tragic catharsis as consisting not in rational insight or in aesthetic (irrational) escape but, rather, in a knowledge which is suprarational, that is, revelation of an absolute or supernatural good. Thus, Weil, unlike her predecessors, proffers an idea of artistic purification which may be regarded as religious rather than philosophical or aesthetic. In opposition to philosophical and aesthetic critics of tragedy, then, Weil may be said to provide a notion of tragedy which offers a basis for arguing in favor of the possibility of a tragedy which is consonant with, rather than antithetical to, a Christian vision of the world.

Weil's idea of catharsis, again, is drawn from the esoteric or mystical rather than the exoteric or rational dimension of Christianity. Mysticism concerns itself with spiritual perfection, perfect selflessness in one's love of God. This love is equated with knowledge.[13] The exoteric dimension of Christianity, on the other hand, is ego-oriented. It concerns itself with merit, won for the self, rather than with loving God without regard to personal benefit. This legalistic facet, one which is necessarily blind to a mystical conception of tragic purification or catharsis, serves as fertile ground for those many theologians, philosophers, and literary critics who deny the possibility of reconciling a tragic with a Christian view of the world.[14]

It would seem that the central problem at issue in the debate about Christian tragedy is the problem of the divine justice. To the discussion of this problem, like to conversation concerning tragic catharsis, Weil brings insight of an esoteric kind. Those who debate the possibility of the existence of a Christian tragedy commonly assume that the Christian outlook espouses a poetic or rational justice whereby the good are rewarded and the evil punished, if not in this life then in an afterlife. This conception of justice presupposes that a Christian God, both all-good and all-powerful, could not act otherwise.[15] This exoteric conception of justice, one which indeed precludes a tragic vision, Weil, a Christian mystic, eschews no less fully than do Aristotle, Hegel, and Nietzsche. She does so, however, on different grounds than they.

For Aristotle, a convenient distribution of reward and punishment is the mark of comedy rather than tragedy. Indeed, the tragic pity central to his idea of the tragic pleasure stems from the spectacle of a hero who suffers a misfortune which is unmerited.[16] Similarly, Hegel eschews the idea that the individual receives his or her just desert in tragedy. In Greek tragedy, for example, a conflict occurs between two persons, each of whom identifies with an ethical position which is fully legitimate but, tragically, partial.[17] The fate each suffers, therefore, is not punishment for a deliberately chosen evil but rather the necessary consequence of his being who he is, of his pathos, a passion which, in a positive sense, he embodies but which as being partial will inevitably conflict with its opposite pathos. Thus, like Aristotle, Hegel also separates tragic suffering from moral desert. Nietzsche opposes poetic justice simply for its moral thrust, as being antithetical to an aesthetic understanding of tragedy, as of life.[18] It would seem, unlike Aristotle and Hegel, that Nietzsche would empty tragedy of moral significance.

Many opponents of Christian tragedy champion the lack of poetic justice in tragedy as a means of exposing the putative naivete of the Christian conception. These thinkers are doubly bolstered by the prevalence of an exoteric conception of Christianity and by the philosophical rather than religious orientation of major tragic theorists such as the three we have examined above. The rational injustice which tragedy enshrines attracts Weil, on the other hand, because she finds in it not a means of exposing the Christian conception but rather a way of purifying it.

A short sketch of the arguments on both sides of the debate concerning whether or not a Christian tragedy is possible will indicate how Weil's own views of tragedy bring to a uniquely satisfying conclusion the central problem at issue in this conversation: the matter of the divine justice.

The definition of tragedy contained in Aristotle's *Poetics* provides a point of departure for many critics of Christian tragedy. "Tragedy," says Aristotle, "is a *mimesis* [imitation] of a high, complete action...in speech pleasurably enhanced, the different kinds (of enhancement) occurring in separate sections, in dramatic, not narrative form, effecting through pity and fear the *catharsis* [purgation] of such emotions."[19] According to Aristotle, then, a human being's fall from happiness to misery, rather than his rise from misery to happiness, provides the most appropriate kind of action for tragic imitation. Further, Aristotle explains, the spectator's pity for the fallen hero springs from a recognition that the hero's calamity is unmerited and the onlooker's fear arises from a sense that the protagonist is a person who is not godlike but, rather, fully human, like himself.[20] According to Aristotle, then, the disaster which a tragedian delineates must be unmerited and of a kind to which any human being might be subject.

Opponents of Christian tragedy claim that the worldview from which the tragic emotions, pity and fear, arise contradicts the Christian concept of the human condition. For these thinkers, divine justice, a central Christian idea, can not reveal itself in tragic art. The tragic emotions, pity and fear, arise from the spectacle of an order of things which regularly causes unjust or innocent suffering.

In a recent, exhaustive study of the debate about Christian tragedy, Barbara Hunt, for example, suggests that the Christian's trust in the existence of an afterlife, his belief that Adam and Eve's sin was a *felix culpa* (happy fault), his faith that the crucified Christ was resurrected—all expressions of faith in a kind of divine poetic justice—render the tragic emotions meaningless. "Because the Christian God is by definition (absolute necessity) just," says Hunt, "his design for man cannot be questioned; therefore, the fall of a Christian protagonist forbids our sympathy."[21]

In a similar vein, Martha Craven Nussbaum, an Aristotelian philosopher, suggests that, for thinkers such as Plato and Kant—philosophers with whom she associates the values of the Judeo-Christian tradition—the pity aroused by tragedy is irrelevant. Aristotle's opponents assert that goodness, the ultimate source of happiness, lies within the domain of human control: "It is evident that this central tragic emotion depends on some controversial beliefs about the situation of human goodness in the world: that luck is seriously powerful, that it is possible for a good person to suffer serious and undeserved harm, that this possibility extends to human beings generally....Aristotle's philosophical opponents...insist that if a person's character is good, the person cannot be harmed in any serious way."[22]

It is commonly pointed out, further, that Aristotle's concept of *hamartia* implies that injustice is an essential ingredient of a tragic vision. Though *hamartia* was often interpreted in a moralistic sense during the Renaissance and the Enlightenment, the term actually refers much more nearly to an error in judgment made by the tragic hero rather than to a flaw in his character, as formerly thought. Thus, if anything, the concept of *hamartia* evokes compassion for the sufferings of the hero rather than justifying them. Any other interpretation, it is pointed out, would jeopardize the central place of tragic pity in Aristotle's interpretation of the tragic effect. The legitimate interpretation of *hamartia* is thus used as further evidence against the consonance of a tragic with a just, a "Christian," vision of the world.[23]

According to the typical opponent of Christian tragedy, then, because the tragic emotions depend on an admission of the universal possibility and the serious importance of unmerited misfortune, they will not influence a true

Christian. According to this idea, an unjust world—a world in which chance perpetually threatens human happiness as well as human goodness—can not be the work of the Judeo-Christian God. This God, they rightly see, is simultaneously all-good and all-powerful. According to these premises, then, the phrase "Christian tragedy" is a simple contradiction in terms.

The critic who seeks to defend the idea of a Christian tragedy, then, must somehow reconcile the notion of a rationally unjust world order, a realm where unmerited misfortune is a universal and a serious possibility, with faith in a God who is at once both powerful and benevolent. The typical defender of Christian tragedy, however, while discovering certain tragic dimensions within Christianity, fails to tackle this central question directly. Those who defend the consonance of the tragic and the Christian worldviews tend to focus on the cross of Christ to the neglect of the problem of creation. In this way the question of God's justice is evaded.

In a rare book-length defense of Christian tragedy, Roger Cox, for example, reveals a certain tragic dimension within Christianity by exploring a kinship between the works of Shakespeare and Dostoevsky, on the one hand, and the writings of St. Paul and the gospel of St. John, on the other. Based on a comparison of these texts, Cox makes the claim that, unlike the moralist, both the tragedian and the Christian sometimes express belief in the possibility and in the central importance of unmerited suffering.[24] Cox, for example, draws a comparison between Aeschylus' idea that wisdom comes only through suffering, by the will of Zeus, and Christ's declaration that he who would follow him must take up his own cross and carry it.[25] Further, for Cox, both the Christian and the tragedian—again unlike the moralist—view the human being as incapable of establishing (or maintaining) his own righteousness by way of rational choice.[26] In this fashion, Cox implies that, with regard to evil, as well as suffering, tragic pity and fear are as relevant for the Christian as for any spectator of tragedy. Yet despite the case that Cox makes for certain tragic aspects of Christianity, by focusing exclusively on the New Testament—a tendency characteristic of writers who defend Christian tragedy[27]—he neglects truly to respond to his opponents. Those who are skeptical about the possibility of Christian tragedy pose a problem which concerns not simply the redeemer but the creator as well. The matter of God's justice, the central issue in the debate about Christian tragedy, can not otherwise be properly discussed.

In accordance with her mystical understanding of the divine, a conception which includes an idea of the creation as well as the cross, Weil discovers a link between the tragic and the Christian visions which confronts directly the central problem of the divine justice. By bringing insights of a mystical or esoteric kind to the problem of the relationship between tragedy and Christianity, Weil may be said to illuminate both the shortcomings of the rationalistic or exoteric approach proposed by the opponents of Christian tragedy and the limitations of the undue emphasis on the New Testament characteristic of its defenders.

As we have seen, the exoteric or rational dimension of Christianity concerns itself with matters of law, merit, and salvation, thereby necessitating a vision of God as a Being who manifests his goodness and his power by distributing reward and punishment according to desert. This view of the divine obviates any vision of a world where innocent suffering is a universal and a serious possibility. The esoteric or suprarational aspect of Christianity, contrarily, concerns itself not with God as a guarantor of justice for men but rather with God as he is in himself, apart from his relationship to the world.[28] Whereas, therefore, exotericism demands a rational idea of the divine justice as a quality which guarantees the fair distribution of reward and punishment, esotericism allows for a view of God's goodness which exceeds rational categories. The mystic aspires to spiritual perfection, to loving God for himself alone, apart from desires for personal benefit. The mystic is not herself concerned with winning God's favor, then, either in this life or in an afterlife. Rather, she strives to know God in his essence. The mystic is thereby able to uncover, by means of a selfless love, a suprarational, rather than a rational, dimension of the divine goodness. This aspect of the divine transcends the idea of rights.

Simone Weil's own conception of God as self-emptying being, a divine kenosis manifested simultaneously in the creation and on the cross, offers an instance of the mystical conception of justice from a specifically Christian perspective. Through the creation of a world which facilitates a mutual self-sacrificial love between man and God, God's goodness, God's justice is made manifest. Simone Weil's religious outlook reveals that a suprarational conception of God's justice, one which may be said to surpass the rational, fully coincides with, rather than contradicts, a tragic vision of the world.

Weil's idea of the divine justice accords in important respects with the concept of God proposed by the theology of the cross, a theology first developed by Martin Luther but revived in recent times in both Catholic and Protestant circles.[29] According to the theology of the cross, the essence of the divine nature can not be known through the works of the natural world or in human moral activity; it can be known only in the cross of Christ and through his sufferings.[30] This revelation of God is essentially an esoteric or hidden revelation. This is a God whose power is concealed in weakness, whose goodness appears as ignominy, whose love arises from out of the depths of affliction and crime. In opposition to all rational conceptions of the divine nature, then, God can not be truly known without knowledge of innocent suffering.

When Christ reprimands Peter for objecting to his Lord's prediction that the Son of Man will soon suffer and be slain in Jerusalem, Christ makes clear that the path of suffering alone is the path of the divine. Suffering also must be the path of anyone who would know the divine. Christ implicitly acknowledges that the way of the cross contains a mystery, a hidden knowledge which human beings do not readily grasp. When Peter indicates, by rejecting his master's prophecy of doom and ignominy for the Son of God, that he believes the way of the cross ought not to be the way of the Christ, Jesus replies, "Get behind me Satan! For you are not on the side of God but of men."[31]

In accord with this important passage from the gospel, and in consonance with a *theologia crucis*, the path to spiritual perfection in Christian mysticism requires participation in the Christ's crucifixion.[32] This participation constitutes a painful dying to the finite self in all its aspects—physical, social, psychological, and even moral. Having a share in Christ's cross constitutes a horrific voiding of the personality in all its natural dimensions. This voiding must occur in order that divine love may dwell within the human soul. From the perspective both of *theologia crucis* and of Christian mysticism, then, any talk of the divine that evokes an image of a God who does not himself suffer or who wields his power over men and women by meting out reward and punishment according to desert, is based on a Christian theology which is false. Only false theology is divorced from knowledge of the cross.

Weil's mystical understanding of the world's creation, an act performed through the mediation of Christ's cross, points to a deeply rooted affinity between the Christian and the tragic visions. God's goodness, rather than excluding, actually necessitates a world where unmerited misfortune is a continual and a serious possibility for every human being. Far from threatening a Christian worldview—as opponents of Christian tragedy contend—the contemplation of unmerited misfortune, an activity which tragedy in the classical tradition promotes, holds the key to understanding Christianity in its essence and in its purity. Meditation on innocent suffering calls to view the impress of Christ's cross in creation.

The two conditions which together may be said to characterize the tragic vision in its classical sense are the same conditions which, for Weil, must be present if a true or perfect love of God may be actuated. According to a Weilian, as to a tragic, vision: (1) The human race, by virtue of its very existence, is subject to blind forces indifferent to the good. These forces take the shape of suffering and evil. (2) Defeat by the exterior world provides the occasion for the human being's greatest victory. This is an inner victory which shines triumphantly in outer darkness.[33]

Simone Weil's Christian vision may be called tragic, then, because, rather than the idea of compensation for virtue, the concept of the human being's interior victory in outer defeat lies at its center. This is a sacrificial notion. Only in a tragic world, a world in which suffering and evil blindly reign, is the human being able to respond to the perfect self-emptying love of God with a perfect love of his own. For Weil, the supreme instance of this love constitutes a participation in the cross of Christ.

According to Weil, the tragic ideal of man's inner victory in outer defeat describes the very purpose for which the human being is created. For Weil, however, only through the mediation of the Christ may the human being achieve inner victory over the world. As history shows, any external victory over suffering and evil, however precious, can be only relative, only partial. However, triumph through Christ's cross is an absolute victory. This triumph is secret rather than public. Ironically, the human being vanquishes the blind sources of suffering and evil whenever her love for the world is absolute. This perfect love only affliction makes possible. The soul who loves in affliction may be said to conquer the world rather than to be conquered by it: She contains within herself a good without condition. This good even the brutal force of necessity, an empire of might which opposes the good by nature, can neither extinguish nor sully.

Wherever the gentle consent to affliction occurs, be it in the soul of atheist or professing Christian, in the heart of ancient Greek or twentieth-century African, this heartbreaking trust constitutes participation in the cross of Christ (*IC*, 184). Thus does the human being respond to the perfect self-renouncing love of God with a perfect love of her own. The unconditional consent to the world's order in affliction, then, constitutes the fulfillment of the highest human aspiration. In tragic phrase, the highest possible inner victory in outer defeat is thus achieved. In traditionalist phrase, the natural self, the ego which always seeks reward for doing good, is purged away and the inner Self is realized. Ultimately, it is because the world order makes possible the Realization of the inner Self, purged of all egoistic desire—and not because the world secures benefits for the virtuous and suffering for the vicious—that it may be said to be good or just.

Weil's esoteric concept of the divine justice, then, offers a legitimate alternative to the exoteric approach common among opponents of Christian tragedy. More specifically, Weil's cosmogony boldly takes to its logical conclusion the often timid assertion of those rare few who defend the possibility of a Christian tragedy by pointing to the cross as an instance of necessary suffering in the heart of Christianity itself. Rather than neglecting the problem of the creation, as these critics do, Weil conceives the act of creation in terms of the cross.

Thus, again, Weil's mystical ideas of the divine justice and of human catharsis (purification) come together in her idea of the world's creation. Affliction leads, through purification or catharsis of the ego, to experiential knowledge of the crucified God. The spiritually purifying consequence of affliction renders the author of a rationally unjust world just on a suprarational plane.

It may be argued that Weil's esoteric theodicy, one inseparable from her mystical view of tragic catharsis, inappropriately superimposes itself upon classical tragedy and, first and foremost perhaps, upon the tragedy of ancient Greece. Greek tragedy, unlike Renaissance and neoclassical tragedy, antedates Christianity. Yet, it would seem that Weil's reason-defying mode of regarding divine justice may shed light indeed on a group of plays that are truly enigmatic. Greek dramas have been proclaimed to be the manifestations of a divinity who lacks any sense of the good, thus providing the subject for only a scandalous or self-destructive theology.[34] At the same time, it has been asserted that a divinity whose justice is undeniable reveals itself not only in the plays of the pious Aeschylus and Sophocles but in those of the skeptical Euripides as well.[35] The image of a cross where divine justice may be regarded as both shocking mystery and priceless boon may indeed cast light on this puzzling body of literature.

Aeschylus and Sophocles, no less than Weil, regard knowledge of the divine as the most blessed human possession. This treasure may mysteriously be attained only through suffering. This kind of affliction can even include moral degradation. Thus, the greatest good cannot be separated from the deepest wretchedness and the vilest ignominy. Justice and accursedness are not separated, Weil suggests, any more in Aeschylus and Sophocles than in the cross of Christ. Thus Weil's esoteric idea of catharsis may be said genuinely to echo the tragic art of ancient Greece.

The theology of Aeschylus and Sophocles itself excludes an idea of the creation. Weil, however, offers a Christian idea of the creation which may account for the kind of heartrending but purposeful world order that these poets describe. Weil's cosmogony may be said to frame Aeschylus' essential idea that fate and the will of God, goodness and brute force, embrace.[36] Might bows in willing obedience to the good, force to divine justice. (Thus the Furies consent to obey Athena through persuasion in the concluding scene of Aeschylus' *Oresteia*.)[37] Equally, Weil's idea of cathartic pain, an affliction the creation purposely enables, may be said to frame the Sophoclean conviction that man's inner greatness, his capacity for self-emptying of the most radical kind, can be actuated only by means of a world order where the potential for calamity reigns.[38]

Far from being a simplifying strategy which would avoid risks, knowledge of an absolute good is achieved only by opening oneself to the universal potential for calamity. This idea opposes the theory of a critic of Greek tragedy such as Martha Nussbaum.[39] Nussbaum, like many modern tragic theorists, rejects a supernaturalist philosophy without perceiving the supernatural underpinning of tragedy itself.

One further point. There are moments in certain Greek tragedies, and in some of their Renaissance and neoclassical imitations, when there becomes revealed the transcendent glory to which the spiritual perfection of the human soul ultimately leads (as the resurrection forms a part no less essential than the passion in the gospel stories). For Weil, however, as for theologians of the cross,[40] it is the moments of pure love, it is the cross, that reveals the essence of the divine nature. A *theologia crucis*, and not a *theologia gloriae* (theology of glory), reveals who God is. In Weilian phrase, through the cross, the divine manifests itself as perfectly selfless heartbreaking love, a love taken to the point of madness. According to Weil, thus, the human being ought to attend Sophocles' *Antigone* or *Oedipus Rex* rather than his *Oedipus at Colonus* or *Philoctetes*; Racine's *Phèdre* rather than his *Esther* or *Iphigénie*; Shakespeare's *King Lear* rather than his *Tempest* or *Cymbeline*. These shocking dramas, unlike the gentler ones, evoke the mystery of Christ's cross. Attending this mystery, Weil believed, could help to center an aimless modern world.

Notes

1. Brémond, *Prière et poésie*, p. 194.

2. On the distinction between the pure and the practical reason of Kant, on the one hand, and the mystic's *fundus animae* or *Seelengrund*, on the other, see Otto, *Idea of the Holy*, pp. 113, 114. For a comparable distinction between reason and Intellect, see Nasr, *Knowledge and the Sacred*, pp. 3–4.

3. For a discussion of the painful or shocking dimension of catharsis in traditional art, see Livingston, *Traditional Theory of Literature*, pp. 99–100. Simone Weil also suggests art may serve a function comparable to spiritual purification, i.e., the purging of the finite self which results in an apprehension of infinite reality (*NB*, 318–19).

4. When Aristotle speaks of tragic insight, he refers to knowledge of a probable rather than an abstract universal (Frederick Copleston, *Greece and Rome. A History of Philosophy: Book One* (1985), vol. 1, pp. 361–62).

5. On Aristotle's virtual omission of the gods in his analysis of Greek tragedy, see John Barbour, *Tragedy as a Critique of Virtue: The Novel and Ethical Reflection* (1984), p. 11.

6. It is possible to assert from the viewpoint of Aristotle's philosophy as a whole that Aristotle had something more sophisticated in mind than simple biological purging when he spoke of tragic "catharsis." In this I agree with Walter Jackson Bate (*Criticism*, p. 18.) For an opposing view, see Copleston, *History of Philosophy: Book One*, vol. 1, p. 367.

7. Anne and Henry Paolucci (eds.), *Hegel on Tragedy* (1962), pp. 28–29, 45–46.

8. On this point see Frederick Copleston, *Fichte to Nietzsche. A History of Philosophy: Book Three*, vol. 7, p. 224.

9. Ibid., p. 198.

10. Friedrich Nietzsche, "The Birth of Tragedy," in *Basic Writings of Nietzsche* (1968), p. 140.

11. Ibid, pp. 23–4, 52, 141.

12. On this point see Barbour, *Critique of Virtue*, p. 28.

13. On esoteric (mystical) knowledge as a function of love (the heart), see Schuon, *Transcendent Unity of Religions*, pp. 159, 163; Underhill, *Mysticism*, p. 84; Johnston, *Inner Eye of Love*, pp. 20, 27.

14. See Roger Cox, *Between Earth and Heaven: Shakespeare, Dostoevsky, and the Meaning of Christian Tragedy* (1969), p. 1: "Philosophers, literary critics, and theologians often contradict each other's conclusions but upon one matter they have reached almost universal agreement—that there can be no such thing as Christian tragedy."

15. The following may be included among the many critics who discount the possibility of Christian tragedy (or who distinguish Christian tragedy from Greek tragedy) on the grounds that, from a Christian perspective, divine justice is a rational justice which manifests itself by punishing the good and rewarding the evil: D. D. Raphael, *The Paradox of Tragedy* (1959); Sylvan Barnet, "Some Limitations of a

Christian Approach to Shakespeare," in *Tragedy: Modern Essays in Criticism* (1963), pp. 199–209; I. A. Richards, *Principles of Literary Criticism* (1925); Preston T. Roberts, "A Christian Theory of Dramatic Tragedy," *Journal of Religion*, vol. 31, no. 1 (1951): 1–20; W. H. Auden, "The Christian Tragic Hero: Contrasting Captain Ahab's Doom and Its Classic Greek Prototype," in *Tragedy: Modern Essays in Criticism* (1963), pp. 234–48; Edmond La B. Cherbonnier, "Biblical Faith and the Idea of Tragedy," in *The Tragic Vision and the Christian Faith* (1957), pp. 23–56; Reinhold Niebuhr, *Beyond Tragedy: Essays on the Christian Interpretation of History* (1937); Karl Jaspers, *Tragedy Is Not Enough* (1952); David Hesla, "Greek and Christian Tragedy: Notes toward a Theology of Literary History," in *Art/Literature/Religion: Life on the Borders* (1983); Richard Sewall, *The Vision of Tragedy* (1959); Northrop Frye *Anatomy of Criticism: Four Essays* (1957); George Steiner, *The Death of Tragedy* (1981).

16. Aristotle, Poetics, in *A New Aristotle Reader* (1987), p. 550.

17. Paolucci, *Hegel on Tragedy*, p. 48.

18. Nietzsche, "Birth of Tragedy," p. 133.

19. Aristotle, *Poetics*, pp. 543–44.

20. Ibid., p. 550.

21. Barbara Hunt, *The Paradox of Christian Tragedy* (1985), p. 126.

22. Nussbaum, *Fragility of Goodness*, pp. 384–85.

23. For a useful sketch of critical interpretations of *hamartia*, see Barbour, *Critique of Virtue*, pp. 2–6.

24. Cox, *Between Earth and Heaven*, pp. 18–19.

25. Ibid., p. 1.

26. Ibid., pp. 34 ff.

27. The following offer examples of the tendency of critics who defend Christian tragedy to emphasize the gospel

narratives to the neglect of the problem of the world's creation: Roger Hazelton, "Tragedy and Providence," *Religion in Life* 31 (1962): 254–63; David E. Roberts, "Christian Faith and Greek Tragedy," *Religion in Life*, 1.18 (1948): 79–88; R. B. Gill, "The Forms of Christian Tragedy," *Bucknell Review*, vol. 26, no. 2 (1982): 74–83.

The proclivity of those who defend Christian tragedy to emphasize the New Testament to the exclusion of the Old Testament may be explained in part by the legalistic conception of justice which predominates in the Old Testament itself. Note, for example, W. Lee Humphreys' comment, "The Hebraic tradition did not produce tragedy in any sustained way or much material informed by tragic vision" (*The Tragic Vision and the Hebrew Tradition* (1985), p. 14).

28. For the general distinction between exotericism and esotericism, I follow chs. 2 and 3 of Schuon, *Transcendent Unity of Religions.*

29. For a useful summary of the recent revival of the theology of the cross in Germany, see Paul S. Fiddes, *The Creative Suffering of God* (1988), pp. 12–13, esp. n. 36.

30. An incisive summary of the essential components of Luther's theology of the cross may be found in Alister E. McGrath's *Luther's Theology of the Cross: Martin Luther's Theological Breakthrough* (1985), pp. 149–51.

31. Mark 8:33, quoted in Johnston, *Inner Eye of Love*, p. 148.

32. On the central role of the cross in Christian mysticism, see Underhill, *Mysticism*, p. 448; Johnston, *Inner Eye of Love*, p. 119.

33. Among those thinkers who regard as central to the tragic vision the notion of inner victory in outer defeat are Krutch, *The Modern Temper*, pp. 123, 124–25; Jaeger, *Archaic Greece*, p. 272; Campbell, *Tragic Drama*, pp. 29–30; A. C. Bradley, *Shakespearean Tragedy: Lectures on Hamlet, Othello, King Lear, Macbeth* (1949), pp. 25–26; Greene, *Moira*, p. 97.

34. Paul Ricoeur, *The Symbolism of Evil* (1967). See esp. pt. 2, ch. 2, "The Wicked God and the 'Tragic' Vision of Existence."

35. Hugh Lloyd-Jones, *The Justice of Zeus* (1971).

36. On Aeschylus' essential idea, see Greene, *Moira*, p. 110. See also Smyth, *Aeschylean Tragedy*, p. 234.

37. Aeschylus, *The Eumenides*, in *The Oresteian Trilogy* (1969), lines 823–976.

38. On Sophocles' fundamental belief, see Greene, *Moira*, p. 98; Jaeger, *Archaic Greece*, p. 283.

39. Nussbaum, *Fragility of Goodness*.

40. See McGrath, *Luther's Theology of the Cross*, pp. 149–51.

CHAPTER THREE

Tragedy of Calamity and the Sacred: *Antigone* and *King Lear*

As we begin now the exegeses of specific tragic dramas, a theory of literature will unfold which strictly contradicts reigning schools of literary criticism. The suprarational interpretations Weil brings to discussions of individual tragedies oppose directly the value-neutral orientation of modernist readings. As the conclusion of this book suggests, however, by its very boldness and originality a traditionalist poetics, of the kind Simone Weil's ideas on tragedy exemplify, may offer hope to a literary world in crisis. Ultimately, modernist value-neutral thought poses a threat to the very cornerstone of literature itself: the act of communication between author and reader. The varieties of poststructuralist literary theory which rule in the present decade violate a writer's and a reader's autonomy, the severest possible effect of relativist philosophy in the world of letters.

At this point, however, modernist readings of classical tragic drama shall hold our attention. The de-moralizing tendency of much contemporary interpretation, an amoral impetus which falsifies the literary works in question, Simone Weil's mystical Christian Platonism helps to reveal.

As we have seen, like all traditionalists, Weil believes that great art will provide an implicit description of the order of things. According to Weil, specifically, in the manner of Plato, the cosmos is constituted of a realm indifferent to the good yet at the same time mysteriously regulated by an ultimate beneficence. Thus, great art, faithful to reality, reflects the secret of the world's justice. The kind of theodicy Weil finds in tragedy is not, then, rational argument. It is, rather, the evocation of mystery. Tragedy offers the sort of justification which the biblical author proposes when he describes Yahweh speaking to the afflicted Job from out of a whirlwind.[1] For Weil, of course, the supreme mystery whose presence the tragic artist implicitly traces is the cross of Christ, a divine self-sacrifice willed from the foundations of the world.

Whereas reason itself acknowledges a mystery as being something above and superior to the rational, a mystery therefore transcending, even as it acknowledges, the distinctions between good and evil; the absurd, on the contrary, appears to reason as being something below or inferior to the rational, failing even to make a significant distinction between good and evil.

It is my belief that classical tragedy of the kind Weil admires points up mystery rather than absurdity, a suprarational good rather than the chaotic or irrational—this, as we will see, in opposition to the assertion of modernist interpreters.

Antigone

Modernists observe the nonrational element in Sophocles' *Antigone* but fail to discern any moral or supramoral dimension. Simone Weil's interpretation of Sophocles, on the other hand, indicates that distinctions between good and evil, as well as the evocation of a suprarational good by which these distinctions are transcended, inform Sophocles' play. Weil's perspective, a traditionalist rather than a modernist one, illuminates particularly the suprarational element of the *Antigone*. Concomitantly, Weil's ideas concerning this play signal an important affinity between the tragic vision and the Christian outlook in its esoteric dimension.

A proper understanding of the conflict between Creon and Antigone, the central substance of the *Antigone*, hinges on interpretations of three passages in particular. The first passage occurs early in the play. Here Antigone evokes the supremacy of divine or unwritten over human or written law. Thus, Antigone defends to Creon her burial of her brother Polyneices, a traitor, in opposition to the edict of Creon who is king:

> It was not Zeus who published this decree,
> Nor have the Powers who rule among the dead
> Imposed such as this upon mankind;
> Nor could I think a decree of yours—
> A man—could override the laws of Heaven
> Unwritten and unchanging. Not of today
> Or yesterday is their authority;
> They are eternal; no man saw their birth.
> Was I to stand before the gods' tribunal
> For disobeying *them*, because I feared
> A man?[2]

The second significant passage occurs toward the end of the play. In these lines Teiresias, a prophet, speaks to Creon. Teiresias makes clear that Creon has issued the edict forbidding Polyneices' burial against the will of the gods:

> Sickness has come upon us, and the cause
> Is you: our altars and our sacred hearths
> Are all polluted by the dogs and birds
> That have been gorging on the fallen body
> Of Polyneices. (979–83)

The third passage precedes the section cited above in which Teiresias utters the pronouncement that vindicates Antigone's burial of her disloyal brother. This third passage is taken from the *kommos*, a dialogue between Antigone and the Chorus. These are Antigone's last words in the play. These lines reveal a disturbed and doubting, yet pious Antigone. Here the young girl takes leave of her fellow human beings just before her execution (the gap between the two sections of the passage, noted here by an ellipsis, contains comments made by the Chorus and Creon):

No chanted wedding-hymn, no bridal-joy,
No tender care of children can be mine;
But like an outcast, and without a friend,
They take me to the cavernous home of death.
What ordinance of the gods have I transgressed?
Why should I look to Heaven any more
For help, or seek an ally among men?
If this is what the gods approve, why then,
When I am dead I shall discern my fault;
If theirs the sin, may they endure a doom
No worse than mine, so wantonly inflicted!
....
O city of Thebes where my father dwelt,
  O gods of our race,
Now at last their hands are upon me!
You princes of Thebes, O look upon me,
The last that remain of a line of kings!
How savagely impious men use me,
For keeping a law that is holy. (891–916)

Interpreters of the *Antigone*, it would seem, fall into two general categories: those who see in the play's central conflict, that between Creon and Antigone, a battle between good and evil, one character therefore regarded as being in the right, the other in the wrong; and those who view this conflict not as an opposition between good and evil but as a tension between two goods, neither character, therefore, viewed as being entirely right or entirely wrong.

The first group of critics I will call "classic" interpreters of Sophocles. By "classic" I mean standard rather than experimental. This group are careful to hold to Sophocles' own, strictly religious worldview. The second set, for their allegiance to W. F. Hegel's reading of the *Antigone*, I will call "Hegelian." The Hegelian readers take less care with Sophocles' original intentions than the classic critics do. Simone Weil, we shall see, harmonizes the classic Sophoclean interpretation with the Christian outlook in its esoteric dimension.

C. M. Bowra's interpretation of the *Antigone* may be taken as an instance of the classic viewpoint.[3] Martha

Nussbaum and George Steiner offer interpretations which are, by contrast, Hegelian.

Typical of the classic interpreter, Bowra explicitly states that Hegel's view is not that of Sophocles, that the play concerns not right vs. right, as Hegel maintained, but rather right vs. wrong.[4] Bowra makes clear also that, generally, in Sophocles, what the gods approve is right and must be accepted and, indeed, that the existence of the gods is what makes conflict between right and wrong central to the work of this tragedian (14). Good and evil are masked for much of the play, however, for whereas Creon's arrogance appears as sincere concern for the state, Antigone's nobility, on the other hand, wears the appearance of self-will (67, 114). Ostensibly Creon issues the edict forbidding the burial of Antigone's traitorous brother as a safeguard for Thebes, which is only just recovering from civil war; on the other hand, Antigone apparently would bury her brother even at the expense of defying the king and therefore the very city in which she lives and which gave her birth.[5]

According to Bowra, the Chorus' own tendency to side with Creon highlights the ignorance to which human beings are naturally susceptible, often mistaking appearance for reality. Here, as usual with Sophocles, according to Bowra,[6] the chorus is not Sophocles' voice (7). The chorus, for example, mistakes Antigone's saintly behavior for a criminal infatuation, the result of a family curse (88). Yet, as the course of events shows, Antigone acts not out of folly at all or frenzied self-will, as it appears, but rather out of clear knowledge of the divine will (88).

The essence of Bowra's interpretation, as of any, I think, hinges on interpretations of the three passages mentioned above: those concerning (1) unwritten law, (2) the prophecy of Teiresias, and (3) Antigone's leavetaking of the Chorus before she is executed.

With regard to the first two passages, both of which concern moral law, Bowra points out that, for the Greek mind, generally, human and divine law were not at odds with one another—indeed, the divine served as a basis for the human (100–1).[7] Bowra suggests Antigone herself knows that the law of the gods serves as the basis of human order and morality. Indeed, as it proves, by violating divine law, it is Creon and not Antigone who jeopardizes the peace of the city after the civil war has concluded. On these grounds, it is difficult to accuse Antigone of a lack of respect for the state, as she is often accused by Hegelians (99).

Sophocles, however, departs from the usual Greek idea concerning the relationship between divine and human law. The tragedian purposely sets the human and the divine at odds, thereby compelling a choice between a political edict, on the one hand, and divine law on the other. The choice Antigone makes, for the average conscientious Greek, is the only one which can be made (100–1). Thus, though for other Greeks the term had a different meaning, for Sophocles, specifically, unwritten law is divine law which must take precedence over human law even in unusual tragic situations where the two are set in conflict with each other. It is precisely in her willingness to honor divine law even at the sacrifice of her own life—a willingness inseparable from her ardent love for her brother, though a traitor—that Antigone's heroism consists. This heroism, Bowra maintains, is felt by us emotionally from the beginning of the play, but it is clearly vindicated only at the end when the gods in fact reveal their will through the prophet, Teiresias (12). Toward the close of the play, as a result of Teiresias' pronouncement against the king's edict, the Chorus warn Creon, in the name of all that is sacred, to bury Polyneices with full rites and to release Antigone whom Creon has wrongly condemned to death.

In the *kommos*, Antigone, suffering deeply, faces fully the fact of her execution. Yet, even here, Antigone continues to assert her humble willingness to acquiesce to the divine will. Antigone asserts this painful attitude of trust, Bowra says, during the very moment when she suggests that her action may have been performed in error (104).

According to Bowra, in the *Antigone*, the gods whose will is revealed through Teiresias, and through Antigone, are not malignant (108–9). Through the suffering brought upon Creon at the end of the play, for example, the gods seek a just retribution for wrong done. Creon had done wrong by forbidding the burial of Polyneices, thereby himself violating a law which allows of no exception, as he did wrong in refusing to relent even when he hears the voice of the people through his son, Haemon, and even, at first, when the gods speak to him through the prophet Teiresias. But the gods seek not only to punish Creon; they also desire to teach Creon modesty, radical humility, or wisdom. The gods hope to instill a knowledge that the human being is a limited creature who must learn reverence for the divine. A spirit of reverence is required from every human being without exception. This requirement binds even a society's king. This, as simple sound theology for the ancient Greek (113).

In contrast with a classical approach such as Bowra's, two contemporary Hegelian interpretations, those of Martha Nussbaum and George Steiner, offer the drama of Antigone and Creon as a function of balanced, unresolved tensions rather than as a battle between good and evil which is ultimately resolved. Initially, it is Hegel who disavows any clear conflict between good and evil in the play. Steiner and Nussbaum adopt Hegel's basic orientation and take it elsewhere, each in his or her own modernist direction.

Unlike a classic critic such as Bowra, Hegel himself explicitly states that Creon is not in the wrong, that he is not a tyrant but a moral power.[8] Hegel views the play's central conflict as that between family (Antigone) and state (Creon) rather than between divine law (Antigone) and human law (Creon). According to Hegel, Creon is a moral voice in the *Antigone*, one well-intentioned though partial in his exclusive concern for the state over the family. Comparably, Hegel suggests, Antigone represents loyalty to the family to the exclusion of civic feeling. For Hegel, the play illustrates a necessary clash between equal, though partial, ethical forces. By means of this clash, according to Hegel, Eternal Justice is vindicated.[9] This play affirms an absolute justice not positively or peacefully, as in Aeschylus' *Eumenides*, according to Hegel, but negatively and through calamity.[10] The destructive conflict the play delineates conveys implicitly the idea that the values of state and family should harmonize and not be put at odds, as they are, tragically, in this play. The *Antigone* is a supreme work of art, for Hegel, because, according to Hegel's philosophy, the harmony of civic and family duty makes for the highest moral life.[11] The *Antigone* illustrates Hegel's own idealist philosophy. The play constitutes one high instance of the Absolute Spirit coming to self-consciousness in history.[12]

Both Steiner and Nussbaum follow Hegel in their general concept of the *Antigone* as a play about tensions between forces which exist on the same level of value rather than as a play about a conflict between values which exist on different planes, one superior to the other. Unlike Hegel, however, both critics believe the tensions generated by the conflict between Antigone and Creon lack any satisfying resolution, even one negatively posed.

In opposition to the classic Sophoclean view, Steiner describes the spirit of Antigone's loyalty to the gods and to her brother as being irrational rather than suprarational. For Steiner, Antigone represents all the irrational forces which the order-loving king, Creon, must oppose. Antigone exhibits a combination of "transcendent irrationality" and "pristine animality."[13] Steiner speaks of Antigone's regard for her brothers' corpses as obsessive, the expression of a primal nocturnal instinct (245). Rather than good beyond the normal or the rational, rather than supernaturally or suprarationally good, as the classic critic suggests, Steiner hints that Antigone's act of burial makes her more primitive than civilized humanity (229).

Steiner sees in the *Antigone* all the principle constants of conflict in the condition of man, all of which he maintains are insoluble, "non-negotiable" (23). Among these he includes the divine and the human. Because Steiner sees the divine and the human as codependent, his view of the play, of course, opposes a classic reading where the negotiated opposition between piety and impiety are of central importance.

In certain ways, George Steiner follows not only Hegel but Aristotle as well. Aristotle himself takes Sophocles' idea of unwritten law to mean a law which is natural rather than supernatural.[14] In a similar spirit, George Steiner interprets Antigone's 'unwritten law' (vs. 'written law') not as divine (vs. human) but rather as subrational or prerational. Sophocles' unwritten law, according to Steiner, reflects an imperative humaneness antecedent to political and social structures (250–51). Steiner claims that Justice (Dike) for Antigone is nature—nature made free of the compromise of time (250), a 'natural eternity' (250) which Steiner associates with death (250). Antigone is, for Steiner, in a condition of timeless (Kantian) ethical imperatives (251), but this condition he associates with sterility, and he cites as a weakness her concomitant denial of eros (273). Eros is that vitality, that life force, to which the categories of good and evil do not apply (258). It is an intensity characterized by "moral extraterritoriality" (258).

In contrast with Bowra, then, according to Steiner, the transcendent absolutes, the unwritten laws Antigone invokes as bases for her action, are essentially secular (270–71). Indeed, it would seem they are value-neutral; for, though her values are those of "humaneness," this is a humaneness which is death-loving and sterile, denying the eternal erotic impulse. This impulse exists outside (not above) the realm of moral categories.

For Steiner, both of the protagonists, Antigone and Creon, by invoking the divine only rarely or indirectly, try to keep the gods at bay (270–72) but fail (276). Rather than viewing Antigone as being at one with the divine will, as in the classic interpretation, Steiner suggests that Antigone, no less than Creon, fights to keep at a distance from the gods. In opposition to a classic view, Steiner describes divinity as an anarchic pressure on civility (269); he regards the "arrival" of the gods as something which necessarily destroys civility and the fabric of reason (276). Steiner concomitantly interprets Teiresias' prophecy as a foretelling of doom for both Creon and his "adversaries" (259). "Adversaries" apparently signify Antigone and those who defend her, such as Creon's son, Haemon. However, the accusatory words of Teiresias themselves, a classic critic would point out, are addressed to Creon alone and not either to Antigone, whom

Creon has wrongly executed, or to his son, who loses his own life for love of Antigone, his betrothed.

For Steiner, then, in contradiction of a classic interpretation, the Sophoclean gods represent all that is hostile to human welfare. They militate against civility. The divine is the irrational which destroys rather than the suprarational which offers an unshakable basis, an eternal, an absolute moral basis, for all human activities including the social or communal. As a concomitant, Antigone, for Steiner, offers an example of what he regards as the heroic temper, something completely secular, the stubborn human will standing alone, self-asserting to the end rather than an illustration of transcendent faith (283).

Even while acknowledging that his interpretation of the *kommos* opposes Sophocles' own worldview, Steiner suggests that in the final scene in which Antigone appears, Antigone entertains the notion that if man is good, he is good in a universe ruled by malignancy (282). Further, again admitting Sophocles did not share the belief he proposes, Steiner asserts that Creon is not impious but rather correct in his suggestion that all human behavior—including Creon's forbidding the burial of Polyneices against divine law—goes unwatched by the gods. To the Sophoclean gods, all human activity, including impiety itself, if there is such a thing, is a matter of indifference (275).[15]

Nussbaum, like Steiner, views the play as a function of tensions which exist on the same level of value. She also, then, in a Hegelian vein, denies the play a hierarchical worldview. Nussbaum faults Hegel for his suggestion that the play teaches us to avoid the kinds of conflicts the play describes.[16] For Nussbaum, conflict itself is something positive, enriching, and, as for Steiner, should be affirmed. Nussbaum, however, follows Hegel in an important way in which Steiner does not. For Nussbaum there is one conflict, not many, in the *Antigone*: the opposition between family and state.

Nussbaum discovers beauty or richness in tension and insolubility, and asserts that any attempt to resolve the conflicts of life results in ugliness or impoverishment. Thus,

Nussbaum's essential vocabulary, it may be noted here at the outset, even despite her own obviously sincere ethical concern, is value-neutral. The best life for her—indeed, the 'good' life, as she terms it—is rich in value, filled with diverse beauties. Nussbaum translates simply as "value" the Greek words for the "good" (*agathon*) and the "beautiful" (*kalon*) (the latter word itself is synonymous with the "noble") (7, note).

Thus, according to Nussbaum, Antigone misses the value of community by committing herself wholly to the concern of family; likewise, Creon's outlook is narrow because he overlooks the significance of family religion. For Nussbaum, these partialities lie not in a necessary onesidedness brought about by a division in the ethical substance itself (Eternal Justice), as for Hegel, but by a personal, essentially cowardly desire to simplify the human experience, to protect oneself from the suffering which conflicts between a multiplicity of values can cause (51).

This assessment of the *Antigone*, of course, opposes the classic critic's idea that the burial of Polyneices, the action which springs from Antigone's absolute devotion to divine law, is good because the gods approve it, whereas Creon's edict, which contravenes that law, is evil because it violates the divine will.

Nussbaum, then, offers Antigone as an example of cowardly withdrawal from conflict. Creon's outlook, too, is narrow and therefore cowardly (66–67). Nussbaum does not ascribe exactly the same degree of cowardice to these two protagonists, however. She cites the slight moral superiority of Antigone. From a classic viewpoint, however, the concession Nussbaum makes misses the absolute difference between good and evil which the actions of Antigone and Creon, respectively, evince.

We may turn, then, to the three passages we have discussed in previous interpretations: those concerning unwritten law, the prophecy of Teiresias, and Antigone's final appearance before she is executed (the *kommos*). As we have seen, in the passage in which Antigone defends her action to Creon, she maintains that the laws she follows are not the written laws, the laws of a mere mortal such as Creon, but rather unwritten laws, the laws of the gods who dwell below, as the laws of Zeus. Rather than interpreting these lines as indications of Antigone's piety, as Bowra does, Nussbaum reads this passage as an indication of Antigone's arrogance (65). Nussbaum believes Antigone mistakenly sets herself up as an arbiter of Zeus' decrees. According to Nussbaum, Antigone is so rigid she misses what piety is all about. Antigone fails to see that true piety admits the possibility of conflict between a plurality of religious duties. The dialogue between Antigone and Creon concerning unwritten and written law is a dialogue between two narrow-minded people. The problem for both characters is that they see their worlds only in terms of a single supreme good and all other values as a function of that good. Both personages fail to see that life offers a multiplicity of goods which exist on the same level of value; they therefore fail to allow for the possibility of painful, perhaps even insoluble, conflicts. According to Nussbaum, the play deliberately juxtaposes these two narrow-minded protagonists as a means of criticizing them both.

Nussbaum shows Aristotelian as well as Hegelian influence. Indeed, the outlook from which she regards tragedy throughout the greater part of her book is Aristotelian. As an Aristotelian, Nussbaum regards ethical matters as practical matters. For Nussbaum, as for Aristotle, the execution of good actions is divorced from knowledge of what is good.[17] Also in keeping with Aristotelian philosophy, Nussbaum posits no Absolute Good, no divine or suprarational good which may be said to transcend natural or human goodness. Given these premises, it is logical that Nussbaum should believe that any overarching commitment to one of many equal goods (all are equal because all are temporal) will be narrowing, a kind of fearful withdrawal into a part as a means of avoiding the whole. As revealed in Sophocles' tragedies, however, at least from the viewpoint of a classic reader, ethics for Sophocles cannot legitimately be viewed as a practical matter; rather, for Sophocles, doing good or evil is inseparable from knowledge of good and evil. Moral awareness itself is unattainable apart from knowledge of the transcendent, the sacred, the divine.

Given her Aristotelian premises, however, it is no surprise that, for Nussbaum, Teiresias appears toward the end of the *Antigone* in order to counsel "practical wisdom" (80). Teiresias' message is not that Creon has offended the gods by refusing to allow Polyneices' burial and, through implication, by having Antigone executed for performing the burial. Rather, Teiresias advises Creon that wisdom lies not in control, the attitude of the single-minded, but rather in yielding, the attitude of the plural-minded (79).

Nussbaum, unfortunately, ignores Teiresias' status as prophet. It is because of the sacred quality of what Creon has dishonored that, at last, only a prophet and not a "layman" such as Haemon, though Creon's own son, can succeed in pointing out Creon's error to him. Thus, Sophocles does not counsel style; he does not counsel yielding or open-mindedness or plurality. Very specifically, Teiresias counsels modesty, reverence for the gods.

Nussbaum regards the *kommos* as a reflection rather of Antigone's cowardice than of her courageous humility. This attitude corresponds with Nussbaum's negative evaluation of Antigone as narrow-minded, like Creon, and therefore, like him, in need of Teiresias' practical advice to yield up a single-minded attitude. In Antigone's final lament to the Chorus—a cry that she suffers as a result of her piety—Nussbaum emphasizes Antigone's address to her audience, the Chorus, leaders of Thebes, rather than the content of Antigone's words themselves. Nussbaum sees here a natural attraction to the communal at the very last. Social concern Antigone has shunned hitherto in a comfortable but single-minded and therefore foolish pattern of avoidance (66).

We will now discuss Simone Weil's comments on the *Antigone* in the context of her traditionalist outlook. Weil's orientation will be seen to be in harmony with a classic rather than a Hegelian reading of Sophocles' play. Because our interest here is Weil's contribution to the debate concerning the possibility of a Christian tragedy, the following discussion will be restricted to the remarks Weil makes on the play from a Christian perspective.[18] As with previous critics, we will comment on the sections of the play which concern unwritten law, Teiresias' prophecy and Antigone's final appearance on stage.

Sophocles' comments on written and unwritten law constitute a central issue in Weil's mature interpretation of *Antigone*. Like classic Sophoclean interpretations of this play, in contrast to Hegelian, Weil interprets written law as human law and unwritten law as divine (although she was aware—and astonished—that some have interpreted unwritten to mean natural: She may have had Aristotle in mind [*TME*, 23]). Unlike the Hegelian, then, in a classic vein, Weil remarks Antigone's clear distinction between the divine and the human. Further, she implicitly reveals the harmony between the classic Sophoclean and the traditionalist worldview, generally, when she discusses this central passage in terms of the concept of the divine which is common to the esoteric dimension of all the religious traditions, that is, the impersonal aspect of God. According to this esoteric conception, the personality is viewed as a privation and, concomitantly, the impersonal as absolute plenitude in God.[19] For Weil, specifically, God is impersonal in the sense of being the divine model of a person who passes beyond the self by renunciation (*WG*, 179). This renunciation constitutes the fullness of love. This idea is in keeping with Weil's generally esoteric but also specifically Christian conception of God as kenotic or self-emptying being and with her idea of the creation as an act not of self-assertion but of self-emptying on the part of God, the creation thus conceived in terms of the cross.

For Weil, the conversation between Antigone and Creon, in which Antigone invokes unwritten over written law, evokes the divine in his impersonal aspect. A God without personality, for Weil, will be a God who is impartial in his love, a God who loves without condition, a God who, like Antigone and in opposition to Creon, would wish the charitable treatment of patriot and traitor alike (*TME*, 23–24). This kind of love, as Creon shows, the realm of the social, does not authorize of itself. Creon himself is rational in his distinctions between good and evil, logically, therefore, wishing to honor the good and punish the evil. This idea is in keeping, it would seem, with the exoteric dimension of Christianity itself. Antigone, on the other hand, is suprarational, wishing to honor the loyal person and the traitorous person alike. According to Weil, the attitude which Sophocles reveals here, an attitude of *caritas*, whereby it is believed that every human being without exception is all-important, distinguishes artistic genius from mere talent (*L*, 104–5).

For Weil, then, the divine in the *Antigone*, contrary to Steiner's depiction, is not irrational. The gods are not, as Steiner has it, immune to the categories of good and evil and therefore enemies of the rational. The divine in Sophocles' play, rather, is a Good which does not deny but which, rather, surpasses that good which is viewed, from a rational perspective, as being the contrary of evil. Where, for Steiner, Antigone's unwritten law is a natural humaneness which precedes human society, something death-loving, sterile, outside reason; for Weil, Antigone's unwritten law, also outside reason, is more nearly like that love, extreme and apparently absurd, which led Christ to the cross (*TME*, 24). Unlike Steiner, thus, Weil speaks of the divine in the same essential manner in which the classic Sophoclean does. She holds up as an ideal that which is not rational but which yet retains the distinctions between good and evil, thereby transcending rather than opposing rational categories.

Before her Christian period, Weil summarizes the *Antigone* for a worker's periodical.[20] After this time, Weil does not discuss the whole play in detail; yet she does attempt to summarize its import. She does so, I think fairly, in one sentence. This statement implicitly makes clear her view of Teiresias' prophecy: "We ought to obey God rather than men" (*IC*, 8). This simple summary sentence confirms that Weil's reading of the play, while Christian, is also classic. In keeping with the classic view that suprarational reconciliation lies at the heart of Sophocles' plays (Bowra) and not irrational conflict (Steiner and Nussbaum), Weil makes useful comparisons between Sophocles' idea of religious mystery and the Christian conception of it. Specifically, as we have seen, Weil explicitly compares Antigone's suffering love to that of Christ on the cross.

In Weil's view, the essence of the cross is supernatural, as opposed to natural, obedience. It is a loving trust, a consent wholly without condition, to an Absolute Good, the divine will. Affliction offers the possibility of transforming natural into supernatural obedience. Supernatural obedience transcends the rational idea of obedience as code keeping. A supernatural consent to obey the divine will is made manifest by a continuing to love the good even in the depths of a torment which rends the soul.

When affliction is endured in a spirit of obedience, this malady has no power over the supernatural part of the soul—the faculty of consent—but it has the power to sever the soul violently from the temporal parts. In this case, although supernatural love dwells in the soul—that is, the unconditional consent to obey the divine will—the sweetness of this love is not felt. It is at such a moment that the soul cries, as the Christ cried out on the cross, "My God, My God, why have you forsaken me?" (*FLN*, 136). In affliction, most of the soul cries, "Stop!" yet one part, infinitely small, yet decisive, has always the power to say, "I consent if divine wisdom so ordains" (*FLN*, 219). So the crucified Christ continued to love the Father perfectly even at the very moment of his heartrending cry.

Weil's comparison of Antigone's affliction to the cross of Christ casts light on the section of the *Antigone* which has been taken by modernists to reveal Antigone's despair[21] or her cowardice[22] or even her heroic stubbornness.[23] All these latter views oppose the classic idea that the *kommos* offers a final revelation of Antigone's sanctity.

In the *kommos*, when Antigone is preparing to be taken to be buried alive in a tomb for violating Creon's edict, Antigone cannot but reflect on her fate, for she is one whose piety has given her the name of impiety. She even doubts, at this point, if she has acted rightly, humbly acknowledging that she may have been wrong, saying that in this matter she awaits enlightenment from the gods.[24] Yet despite this near despair, Antigone never ceases to love the good; this is revealed by the fact that never in her own moment of dereliction does she repent the act, the utterly self-sacrificial act, by which she gave her brother sacred burial; nor does she repent her faith in the gods.[25]

In the period following her immersion in the Christian inspiration, Weil speaks of Antigone's humiliation as a feeling of abandonment. Weil says here that Antigone perishes for loving beyond reason. Antigone stops the curse on the house of Labdacus because she is a pure victim obedient to God (*IC*, 10). All these comments reverberate Weil's central statement, indicated previously, that the love which prompts Antigone to bury her brother, according to the will of the gods, at the sacrifice of her own life, resembles that love extreme and apparently absurd which led Christ to the cross. Thus, an indestructible inner freedom which Weil believes is characteristic of the Sophoclean hero, one which Weil speaks of in earlier years (*FLN*, 49), takes on a specific content after her conversion at Solesmes. It becomes now the capacity for suprarational love, the mystic's consent to obey, the substance of the perfect love of Christ for the Father on the cross, even at the moment of abandonment.

The movement of catharsis in the *Antigone*, then, according to a Weilian reading, is Antigone's own purification in the *kommos*. In this, the final scene in which she appears, the heroine is emptied of all security and self-regard. Yet she does not lose a love of the good. Here, specifically, that good constitutes an act she herself performed: the burial of her brother, Polyneices. By the act itself, as by her refusal to repent it, Antigone bears witness to the supernatural good which undergirds moral law.

Any exoteric interpretation of this play will find no justice in it, as any exoteric conception of God will not be satisfied by it and will declare the *Antigone* to be at odds with the Christian as any religious worldview. Though the wicked suffer and come to see the wrong they have done (Creon), in the *Antigone*, the good are not rewarded. Antigone, though vindicated by Teiresias, dies before Creon's belated and repentant rescue. She perishes ignorant of her honor in the eyes of her fellow human beings and uncertain of it in the eyes of the gods. But tragedy does not offer, nor does the esoteric dimension of Christianity seek, poetic justice. Tragic theodicy offers a justice, a good which transcends reason and the good and evil which reason perceives as opposites. From Weil's perspective, one which is not identical to but which yet is consistent with a classic Sophoclean view, the Good the *Antigone* affirms is the suprarational good, the love to the point of madness, which undergirds the very order of the world.

To the undiscriminating, divine love which Antigone invokes in the passage concerning unwritten law—an eternal law that affirms the value of the life of every human being (good or evil)—Antigone offers a responsive echo when she herself loves the divine without condition. She executes the divine law at the cost of her life and even refuses to repent her action when, in the manner of the crucified Christ, she believes herself to have been personally rejected by the gods hopelessly and without cause. Thus, the forces that lead the innocent Antigone inexorably to her doom are actually and mysteriously a function of the good. Without these negative forces, the utterly unconditional, the suprarational quality of Antigone's own love could not be or exist.

Thus Weil's religious metaphysics illuminates the central idea in the *Antigone*. It is an idea which the Hegelian simply overlooks, though the plot of the drama itself serves to reveal it: Antigone's will and the divine will are at one.[26] Concomitantly, Weil illustrates an important point of contact between the tragic vision and the Christian vision in its esoteric dimension.

The play offers, likewise, an illustration of Weil's theory of art, whereby a truly sacred work of art will imitate the world's order. This order contains a dual nature—one at once indifferent to the good (hence the existence of affliction, a consummate misery such as Antigone endures) and mysteriously complicit with that good (hence the human being's ability to refuse to surrender an attitude of gentle love even in affliction, as Antigone refuses to do). For Weil, the supernatural good to which Antigone at first bears witness and later assimilates herself by imitation constitutes divine love, a love utterly without condition. This mysterious good is evoked, then, in the passage concerning unwritten law, confirmed by the prophecy of Teiresias and exemplified in the *kommos*. This is the mysterious element which provides a theodicy to the play, one beyond the rational in any form, religious (exoteric) or secular (philosophical).

King Lear

Shakespeare's *King Lear* imitates a suprarational love. This love is characterized by the hero's unconditional acceptance of a heart-rending fate. *Lear*, like *Antigone*, may be called a high tragedy with a Christian tone.

As in Sophocles' play, the suprarational in *King Lear* reveals itself as the mysterious, supernatural good which, though not identical with moral good, yet undergirds and sacralizes moral law. The bond between parent and child, rather than the right to burial, constitutes the moral law at the heart of conflict in *King Lear*.

I believe two passages of *King Lear* are of particular importance: (1) Lear's first words in the play's last scene and (2) Lear's final words in that same scene. In both sections Lear expresses his love for his youngest daughter, Cordelia.

At the outset of the play the aging king determines to divide his kingdom among his three daughters in exchange for professions of their love for him. Cordelia alone refuses to mix her love for her father with material things, as Lear desires her to do. Mistaking her reticence for lack of affection, Lear banishes Cordelia, choosing thus her elder sisters as the nurses of his age. Unlike Cordelia's, the love of her two sisters is eloquent but untrue. Humiliation, madness, and despair, provoked by his two daughters' abuse, teach Lear gradually the value of the filial tie he has cut. Cordelia herself soon learns of her father's abuse at her sisters' hands. As bride of the King of France, Cordelia enlists the French army on the king's behalf. British forces, however, defeat the French. As the final scene of the play opens, Lear and Cordelia face defeat at the hands of Edmund, Earl of Gloucester. Lear addresses the following words to his daughter as they are ordered to prison:

> ...Come let's away to prison:
> We two alone will sing like birds i' th' cage;
> When thou dost ask me blessing, I'll kneel down
> And ask of thee forgiveness. So we'll live,
> And pray, and sing, and tell old tales, and laugh
> At gilded butterflies, and hear poor rogues
> Talk of court news; and we'll talk with them too—
> Who loses and who wins; who's in, who's out—
> And take upon's the mystery of things
> As if we were God's spies; and we'll wear out,
> In a wall'd prison, packs and sects of great ones,
> That ebb and flow by th' moon.[27]

The second significant passage Lear utters as Cordelia (hanged by the order of Edmund) lies dead in his arms shortly after their removal to prison:

> And my poor fool is hang'd! No, no, no life!
> Why should a dog, a horse, a rat, have life,
> And thou no breath at all? Thou'lt come no more,
> Never, never, never, never, never.
> Pray you undo this button. Thank you, sir.
> Do you see this? Look on her! Look her lips,
> Look there, look there! *He dies.*
> (V.iii.306–12)

The central critical debate concerning *King Lear* has been articulated in terms of the degree to which the play may be called "pagan" and pessimistic, on the one hand, or Christian and optimistic, on the other.[28] This concern to determine the pagan or Christian nature of the play itself hinges primarily on an interpretation of the play's final scene. Weil's comments on *Lear*, as her outlook on tragedy, generally, will help to reveal the mistaken nature of the terms in which this debate has been cast. For, as we have seen, it is not optimism (a rationalistic term) but mystery which marks the authentically Christian work of art. Weil's equating the Christian viewpoint with a theodicy of mystery illuminates particularly the all-important final scene.

A. C. Bradley well illustrates the problem at the heart of the debate about the pagan or Christian nature of Shakespeare's play when he underscores the shock of its ending. In opposition to the explicitly Christian *Chronicle of King Leir* on which the play is apparently based, Shakespeare does not, as the author of the *Chronicle* does, allow Cordelia and Lear to live after they have become reunited through a long struggle. As Bradley points out, by play's end Cordelia has been murdered almost by a quirk of fate;[29] also, Lear has died from loss of her. The question of the play's justice, the question of moral order, hinges for most critics, therefore, on the final scene. The events of act V, generally, seem simply to reverse the upbeat tone of act IV in which Lear and Cordelia are first united, at long last, in mutual understanding and love. This reunion turns the first scene of act I around, where Lear had mistakenly chosen his elder daughters as the minders of his age and banished the one daughter who loved him truly. How can such an ending, thus, conclude a play over whose world a just providence may be said to reign? How can such a play be regarded as Christian, a drama which provides a satisfactory theodicy?

From the perspective of the religious traditions, the suprarational aspect of the good, its mystery, alone can provide a satisfactory sense of justice to any artistic vision. The suprarational or supramoral, however, cannot be perceived in a context that excludes the categories of good and evil. Yet modernist critics of *King Lear* tend to exclude moral categories from their field of vision, in the same manner as modernist critics of *Antigone*. Indeed, critics of this play may be divided according to those who emphasize and those who bypass the drama's concern with moral law. Primarily, William Elton's interpretation will be offered as an example of the modernist, value-neutral approach to the play; Roy Battenhouse and Martin Lings will furnish examples of the moral orientation. As we will see, from the perspective of Simone Weil, the supernatural both affirms and transcends moral law in *King Lear* no less than in the *Antigone*. The affliction of Shakespeare's central character constitutes a catharsis which reveals the mark of Christ's cross. In this sense *King Lear*, like the *Antigone*, furnishes a theodicy of mystery.

Any interpreter who asserts that ambiguity or lack of definite meaning characterizes *King Lear* cannot at the same time maintain that the play holds distinctions between good and evil at its core. Critics such as Stephen Booth or Robert Hunter, in a romantic vein, for example, suggest that artistic patterning or aesthetic insight offers a compensation or adequate substitute ("religious" in kind) for what these two thinkers call a lack of moral vision in the play. Aesthetic compensations, both critics argue, are necessitated by Shakespeare's ambiguous treatments of major themes. Nicholas Brooke, another modernist critic, maintains that *King Lear* lacks aesthetic as well as moral compensation.[30]

William Elton, an influential student of tragedy and Christianity, though not precisely romantic or nihilistic in outlook, also interprets Shakespeare's play as being amoral in tone. Elton argues that King Lear himself ultimately offers an example of skepticism as the Renaissance knew it. Philosophical skepticism is an outlook defined in large part by naturalist philosophy. The naturalist holds that no essential distinction exists between man and beast (180, 190–91ff.). According to Elton, Shakespeare's Edmund, Son of Gloucester, exhibits a naturalist outlook from the beginning of the play. Gradually, through experience, Lear himself manifests the same view. Lear's psychological move from faith to skepticism constitutes the most significant dynamic of the play (335–38).

Elton thus portrays King Lear as victim and rebel in relation to irrational cosmic powers. In the process, unfortunately, Elton glosses over the plot of the play. The play's action concerns a father's discovery of his own infidelity to his one faithful daughter.[31] Elton interprets Lear's suffering, for example, not as a function of his having disowned his one loyal daughter in favor of her untrue sisters but rather as unjust and meaningless punishment for eighty years of faithful service to his gods (216). Elton regards Lear's anguish as an education in cosmic cruelty (218), a 'revelation' that law lacks any transcendent sanction (230).

Lear's initial reunion with Cordelia in act IV of the play Elton regards as an essentially irrelevant interlude in Lear's "Promethean" protest against the world's order (239). Similarly, Elton compares the prison Lear describes in the pivotal prison speech of the play's final scene to a cage "borne about for unacknowledged purpose by those greater mysterious powers which imprison man" (240). The vision of happiness itself, contained in the prison speech, Elton sees as an illusion, a wishful escape (240). Further, Elton discovers blasphemous overtones in Lear's assertion that, while in prison, he and Cordelia will take upon themselves the mystery of things (250). In the course of the play, Lear does not violate the tie between parent and child and then repent the violation; rather, he undermines the bond itself (132). Thus, Elton argues, Lear's "Why?" at Cordelia's death, is the "Why?" of the philosophical skeptic (55).

As a result of the shocking end of the play—an end Elton asserts Shakespeare has prepared us for by Lear's gradual loss of faith in the gods from act I forward—no benevolent providence can be shown to be operative, no "watchful God who rewards good and punishes evil" (42). In conclusion, Elton asserts, no Christian interpretation of the play is tenable.

Contrary to a reader such as Elton, Roy Battenhouse links Lear's suffering with his moral character. Battenhouse makes this connection, of course, with particular reference to Lear's treatment of Cordelia. Elton interprets the famous cry Lear utters during the storm into which his two older daughters have cast him—"I am a man more sinned against than sinning" (III.ii.59–60)—as an insight into his own increasing victimization by cosmic powers (261). Battenhouse, on the other hand, views this assertion as a false, self-justifying claim. This cry is heard no more, Battenhouse points out, once Lear both learns modesty and gains insight into the weaknesses of his own character through his experience of helplessness against the elements.[32]

According to Battenhouse, Lear's deepest torment, his madness, can be traced to vanity. His self-conceit reveals itself most clearly in the opening scene when Lear mistreats Cordelia by coveting an infinite love for himself at any cost: "For in his vanity he begets a bastard kind of justice which becomes an instrument for cutting his own brains with madness" (277). By the very end of the play, through suffering, Lear's egotism has transformed itself into generosity: Calamity has refined selfishness away (292–93).

Battenhouse offers Lear's final lines (V.iii.306–12) as support for, rather than evidence against, the existence of a providence at work in Lear's world. Significantly, Battenhouse compares Lear's last words with the scene in which Lear and Cordelia are first reunited (IV.vii). Battenhouse suggests that Lear's "Look there, Look there," indicates not illusion that the murdered Cordelia is alive mysteriously, despite appearances, as some critics maintain (290). These words manifest a move toward hope and love of an authentically supernatural kind: "The verbs as carriers of action have cycled upward. We need not claim that they signalize, at the end of this psychological claim, a Lear completely assured of a resurrected life in Cordelia, but rather that his love-impelled reason is converging toward and verging on such a faith beyond reason. A dream of new life is summoning him—as, indeed had been his experience once before, when he awoke to an imagination of Cordelia as 'a soul in bliss' yet qualified that judgment with the contention, 'I fear I am not in my perfect mind.' Lear's bewilderment in both episodes (the one in act IV, the other at the play's end) seems to me to picture a mind groping toward supernatural fact" (290).

Battenhouse suggests that after the scene of initial reunion between father and daughter (IV.vii), there can be but one further step for Lear: the complete renunciation of self when Cordelia dies (V.iii.306–12). Thus Battenhouse discounts any spiritual significance for the prison speech which comes between the two sections.

Despite Battenhouse's belief, contrary to more skeptical critics, that Lear's very final words imply a suprarational faith rather than illusion, this Christian critic stops short when it comes to maintaining that Shakespeare's play offers an actual vision of a transcendent good.[33] This critic thus fails, from a traditionalist perspective, to offer a theodicy of mystery or therefore satisfactorily to reconcile this tragedy with a Christian vision.

Martin Lings, unlike Battenhouse, argues that *King Lear* reveals Christian truth in its esoteric or mystical dimension. Yet, though his interpretation resembles Weil's in this regard, unlike Weil, Lings does not suggest the play evokes the central Christian mystery, the cross of Christ.

The drama of Lear is for Lings less a drama of sin, forgiveness, and salvation than it is a play of sanctification. In this play, knowledge of good and evil, while existent, is transcended to include knowledge of a good absolute in kind. When Lear is banished to the heath by his heartless daughters, set free of worldly ties, then the unsettling of his wits marks a turn toward wisdom.[34] But the wisdom Lear gains is not merely new knowledge of the selfishness in his soul, hitherto concealed from him. The understanding Lear attains is in part moral, but it is also supramoral, suprarational. For Lings, the prison speech is a pivotal passage. This speech reveals a contemplative objectivity, the opposite of Lear's former undiscriminating, undetached, and feverish subjectivity (80). The chief wisdom to which Lear attains in this passage is a revelation of the beauty and thereby the harmony of the universe. These lines thus justify the ways of God to man. They do so not by an appeal to reason but through an evocation of mystery (136).

Lings thus sees mystery in the prison speech where Elton sees only irrationality or absurdity. This momentary glimpse into the world of holiness does not last, Lings acknowledges, but it makes an imprint on the soul (138). As Shakespeare reveals in the prison speech, only God's spies can perceive God's justice, the justice of providence (138). It is not blasphemous—as Elton maintains—but rather holy to find oneself possessed of this knowledge. Thus, by the time of the prison speech, knowledge of good and evil exists, but this understanding no longer screens an Absolute Good. At play's end, then, we no longer ask ourselves, Why does God allow evil?, for we have mysteriously apprehended the answer to the question on a supprarational plane (139). In addition to this suggestion that the play offers a satisfying answer to Lear's "Why?" at Cordelia's death, Lings also proposes that the close of the play evokes eternal life (81). Apparently, Lear's mysterious "Look there, look there" constitutes the basis for this latter suggestion.

Like Lings, Simone Weil suggests *King Lear* offers a vision of Good which simultaneously contains and transcends the rational distinction between good and evil. This is a Good which specifically, for her, however, is the cross of Christ. At one point, Lings briefly suggests Shakespeare has the cross of Christ in mind when he describes the loving sacrifice of Cordelia on behalf of her father (80–81). Weil's comments on the play, however, offer the basis for an interpretation which places this most important Christian mystery in a central place. Weil implies the deep influence of Christian mystery when she suggests that Lear himself suffers an affliction comparable in certain respects to that of the crucified.

First we will peruse Weil's comments on *King Lear*, as a whole, including her comments on Lear's final words. These preliminary comments will prepare the ground for unveiling the image of the cross at the heart of this play. A Weilian interpretation of the prison speech, finally, will reveal the cruciform nature of the universe which Shakespeare's play imitates.

Weil quotes six passages from *King Lear* which she believes contain "the very essence of the tragedy" (*L*, 103). Rather than the excerpts most commonly cited by Christian interpreters—those that indict Lear's immoral behavior or describe his moral progress, or those that evoke an after-life—Weil quotes exclusively lines that reveal Lear's suffering. In these passages, Lear feels the helplessness of old age, fear of madness, shame, emotions which more than once, against his will, cause him to weep. Through the passages she quotes, Weil illustrates Lear's humiliation at the hands of his daughters Goneril and Regan (five of the six quotes, taken from acts I, II, and III); and his despair at the death of his one beloved child, Cordelia (the final quote, taken from V.iii.306–12).[35] None of these passages refers to Lear's sinfulness or pride, vanity or covetousness, but only to his brokenness. Weil does not deny Lear's sinfulness, but, unlike moralistic critics, she draws attention to his sinfulness as shame, a form of suffering, rather than as wrongdoing. "Helplessness—I do not mean weakness of character, but utter lack of material force—breathes forth in these lines all its bitterness. For it is bitter, nothing in the world is so bitter." Weil continues, "Yet it is better for the soul than triumph and power, because there is truth in it; it is not, like these, poisoned with delusion and lies" (*L*, 104). And yet a suffering like Lear's, one intimately mixed with helplessness and self-contempt, though containing more truth than a certain kind of happiness (the kind which causes self-satisfaction), cannot be man's destiny. On this account, Weil says, though "the vilest prostitute in the streets, is better than a self-righteous woman born in a rich family, still such misery is shameful; the soul yearns for a truth not mingled with misery, shame and bondage, and dares not think it can't be found in this world. I believe it can" (*L*, 104).

The truth unmingled with shame, bondage, and misery, for Weil, is the suprarational good which the crucified Christ continues to long for and to love even in the depth of his affliction. The misery of Lear Weil explicitly compares to that of the Christ at the moment of forsakenness. Weil asserts in her comments on Lear's suffering, "It was not until Christ had known the physical agony of crucifixion, the shame of blame and mockery, that he uttered his immortal cry...My God, why hast thou forsaken me? When poetry struggles toward the expression of pain and misery, it can be great poetry only if that cry sounds through every word" (*L*, 103).

The "Why?" of Lear's final words to the murdered Cordelia, "Why should a dog, a horse, a rat have life and thou no breath at all?" (V.iii.307–8) is not, as Elton maintains, the skeptic's why, not something philosophical or theoretical. It is, more nearly, the cry of the crucified Christ, the why that comes out of the depths of the entire being, the eternal cry of the soul. This is a moan that finds its way through all the crimes the soul has itself either suffered or committed, a mourning that expresses pained surprise that evil is done to one and not good. Yet, during this cry, the soul never renounces love for that very good which it longs for and does not receive (*TME*, 14). Lear sounds the loving note of his anguish, mutely, during the storm on the heath when the abuse of his daughters Goneril and Regan literally drives him mad with humiliation and helplessness (act III) and, vocally, in the final scene, when his beloved Cordelia lies dead in his arms (V.iii.258ff.). Once engendered (II.iv.266–72), Lear's repentant love of Cordelia never wavers. Either during the storm or just before he dies. Thus, even in the depths of his affliction, Lear's love of the good triumphs. So Weil suggests by her explicit comparison of Lear to the crucified.

I believe the prison speech, a passage Weil herself does not quote, offers evidence in support of Weil's contention that Shakespeare's play evokes the cross of Christ. Here, I suggest, the very object of the crucified's loving cry is itself described. In this respect, the passage is comparable to Antigone's evocation of unwritten law and Teiresias' vindication of her claim. If the significance of the prison speech is to be understood, however, the passage must be placed within the context of a Weilian reading of the play as a whole.

As we have seen, in the opening scene of Shakespeare's play, King Lear offers his daughters portions of his kingdom in exchange for professions of their love for him (I.i.36–54). From the perspective of a limited dualism which is specifically Christian, this gesture bespeaks a mistaken belief that the good and the necessary, love and the world, belong to the same order. Though she is herself, of course, no conscious metaphysician, Cordelia alone of his three daughters believes her father's bargaining rests on a grievous error. Taking his ignorance to heart, she remains silent when he asks for her declaration of love (I.i.62, 87, 89). Cordelia's defiant silence implies a belief that the secret, the suprarational nature, of love is hidden by right and ought not to be forced into the open; it ought not to be mixed with the things of the world. Finally, however, Cordelia replies that she loves her father according to her bond as daughter, no more, no less (I.i.92–93). This bond is a sacred bond which will not brook violation. Lear is ignorant of the sacred quality, the suprarational element, of the tie which joins parent and child. When he compares Cordelia's simple words to her sisters' flattering speeches, he therefore mistakes Cordelia's reply for the sign of a lack of affection, heartless, insubordinate pride (I.i.106, 108–19). In this same manner, Creon mistakes Antigone's defiant assertion of the sacred nature of the duty to bury the dead for an insubordinate threat to his own authority.

When Lear's two foolish daughters, who merely flatter their father in the opening scene, cast Lear out into a storm shortly after he has disowned Cordelia, Lear finds himself stripped of all respect, power, and dignity. No longer a strong, secure, and beloved king, Lear finds himself, rather, wholly abandoned to the elements (III.i–vi). Thus Lear begins to suspect the falsity of the premise by which he had judged his children. It is not so much that selfishness will turn to selflessness through suffering, as a moralistic Christian critic might imply, as that through suffering Lear's ignorance will turn to knowledge, a twofold knowledge. The experience of extreme affliction will yield Lear knowledge of the good as well as the necessary. The former is the secret of a supernatural realm, the latter the essence of nature. The mystery of the mediation which exists between these two spheres Lear will both apprehend and actualize. The secret of this bridge between realms is more frightful than a gibbet, as blessed as a cross.

In a remark to Gloucester's son, Edgar, whom he encounters on the heath during the storm, Lear illustrates what his fall from comfortable kingship into affliction is beginning to teach him about the nature of this world. To the beleaguered, naked Edgar, an apparent madman, Lear says, "Thou art the thing itself; unaccommodated man is no more but such a poor, bare forked animal as thou art" (III.iv.105–7). Affliction teaches Lear that the distinctions the world makes between human beings, high and low, king and outcast, are meaningless; all persons are but two-legged beings exposed to forces indifferent to the good; variations between them are the result of pure accident. This understanding evokes not cynicism but compassion.

During the storm Lear feels sincere pity for the wretched of the world for the first time. He learns through affliction a fact of which his security and power as king had kept him ignorant. The harsh truth unfolds that a blind and pitiless necessity rules this earth and all the people in it: "Poor naked wretches, wheresoever you are, / That bide the pelting of this pitiless storm, / How shall your houseless heads and unfed sides, / Your looped and windowed raggedness, defend you / From seasons such as these? O, I have taken / Too little care of this! Take physic pomp; / Expose thyself to feel what wretches feel" (III.iv.28–36).

As his newborn love of neighbor attests, once Lear has been schooled in the ways of the world, like a prisoner in a cell who fastens himself to a window, he directs his horrified heart away from temporal things, including, therefore, all those things which make up rank and fortune. Indeed, by the final scene of the play, though briefly, Lear actually beholds a separate reality. This vision is new for him; it has been violently induced by the wisdom only affliction can bring.

Throughout the time of his affliction Lear courageously sustains a longing for the good. This desire is manifested by a repentant attitude toward Cordelia. After this repentant feeling is engendered, during the time of Goneril's abuse (II.iv.266–72), it never wavers. Lear does not speak of Cordelia during the storm. His affliction chains his thoughts down to the source of his misery, the ingratitude of the children who banished him from their hearths. But we know Lear loves Cordelia now. This is a love Lear never disavows. Yet this love in affliction actually has not a human but rather a superhuman object. An absolute good undergirds and sanctifies the prodigal father's tie to his daughter.

Lear reveals his vision of the supernatural to Cordelia as father and daughter face defeat together at the hands of Edmund. At this point in the play, Lear perceives the true nature of the bond that joins him with Cordelia: Her forgiveness in the previous act had been only a dim experience when he was just recovering from madness (IV.vii.43–83).

Before the time of his affliction, Lear had thought the order of the world was benign rather than pitiless. When

Lear had asked for professions of love from his daughters in exchange for portions of a kingdom, he had betrayed a mistaken belief that love and the world operate according to the same laws. When the king had rejected as insufficient Cordelia's declaration that she loved him as a child is bound to love a parent, no more or less, Lear had not known the absolute quality of the love that characterizes human bonds. Now, as he and his daughter together face imminent destruction at the hands of enemy powers, Lear perceives that a whole separate reality undergirds the relationship between his daughter and himself. This realm transcends the rule of fickle fortune:

> ...Come, let's away to prison:
> We two alone will sing like birds i' th' cage:
> When thou dost ask me blessing, I'll kneel down
> And ask of thee forgiveness. So we'll live,
> And pray, and sing, and tell old tales, and laugh
> At gilded butterflies, and hear poor rogues
> Talk of court news; and we'll talk with them too—
> Who loses and who wins, who's in, who's out—
> And take upon's the mystery of things
> As if we were God's spies; and we'll wear out
> In a wall'd prison, packs and sects of great ones,
> That ebb and flow by th' moon. (V.iii.8–18)

In his struggle to understand the meaning of the bond between parent and child, Lear discovers the face of love behind the veil of the world. Lear knows, in the final scene, what he did not know at the play's opening: The kingdom of love is not of the world. The realm of the heart exists separately and secretly. Love should not, therefore, be conditioned by earthly things, as Lear had tried to condition the bond between himself and his daughters by offering worldly advantage in exchange for devotion. At last, the old king discovers that, however blind the order of the world may appear, a secret realm gives meaning, sanctification, and blessing to the natural order, including natural relations. These relations include the bond which unites a parent to a child.

The prison speech is the only passage in the play which reveals the good in its supernatural aspect. These lines constitute the infinitely small but decisive point in *King Lear* which imitates the very order of the world. The supernatural love described here is the good for which Lear longs when, during the storm, in the depths of affliction, his heart, nearly broken, cries forth, "My God, my God, why have you forsaken me?" The real object of his heart's longing is revealed to Lear only at the time of his prison speech. For a brief moment, then, the old king is released from the chains of the necessary, the manacles of suffering and all we call evil, the forces which shackled him on the heath and which will resume their hold soon. Here the reader apprehends the suprarational object of the loving cry of dereliction which, Weil suggests, pierces through the very heart of Shakespeare's play.

Many Christian interpreters offer "Look there, Look there" (V.iii.312) as a mysterious note of hope in a world beyond. Or these words are offered as evidence that Lear dies believing Cordelia still lives. The verses from the final speech which Simone Weil cites, however, are the ones more often emphasized by modernist than Christian critics: "Why should a dog, a horse, a rat have life, / And thou no breath at all?" (V.iii.307–8). As these words show, at the end of the play, when Lear holds the dead Cordelia in his arms, Lear sustains an attitude of love. The heartbreaking quality of that love, culminating in this shattering question, Lear vocalizes now. The king's crucified heart had remained mute during the storm when filial ingratitude stole away his mind. Lear thus maintains unremittingly a love for the good in the depths of his affliction, whether silently or in words.

The close of Lear's story constitutes the ending of a tale which reveals the impress of Christ's cross. The story of Lear thereby furnishes a theodicy of mystery. Lear's drama evokes the eternal love of the crucified Christ for the Father during the moment when the Christ believes he is personally bereft of the Good forever.

The theodicy of mystery contained in the *Antigone*, we remember, depends first on the evocation of the suprarational supplied both by Antigone's vocalized faith in unwritten law and by Teiresias' vindication of that faith. The play's justification of the world's order depends secondly on Antigone's assimilation to the supernatural good itself, a good beyond reason. This assimilation Antigone achieves through a purification from all earthly ties. Antigone's suffering illustrates a catharsis which results in spiritual perfection. This perfection Weil regards in Christian terms as a love which is perfectly self-emptying. Antigone never ceases to love the good even during her moment of dereliction. This triumph is manifested when she holds fast to her sacrificial act of burial amidst the severest duress.

Similarly, the theodicy of mystery evoked in *King Lear* first depends on the prison speech, Lear's poetic description of a suprarational good. Secondly, the shadow of a suprarational justice rests on the protagonist's severing from all earthly ties, the purifying process that enables assimilation to a good which is absolute. The painful catharsis begins during the storm into which Goneril and Regan cast their father, and culminates in the moment of mourning for the hanged Cordelia just preceding Lear's death. During the deepest times of his affliction, Lear, like Antigone, never relinquishes a love for what is good. The darkness never extinguishes Lear's repentant love for Cordelia, once the bright light is lit.

We remember, for Weil, the order of the world came into being through the mediation of Christ crucified. The creation itself, therefore, bears eternally the stamp of the cross. This impress only art of the highest genius reflects.

Notes

1. See Otto, *Idea of the Holy*, p. 79.

2. Sophocles, *Antigone*, in *Sophocles: Three Tragedies* (1964), lines 440–450. Further references to the *Antigone* will be to this edition and will be documented in the text.

3. The following critics, like Bowra, offer "classic" interpretations of the *Antigone*: Victor Ehrenberg, *Sophocles and Pericles* (1954); Karl Reinhardt, *Sophocles* (1979); James C. Hogan, *A Commentary on the Plays of Sophocles* (1991).

4. Bowra, *Sophoclean Tragedy*, pp. 65–66. Page numbers of further references to *Sophoclean Tragedy* will be found in parentheses after each citation.

5. Weil herself suggests that there hangs a transparent veil of truth over this play (*FLN*, 195).

6. Hogan agrees that Sophocles does not voice his own attitude through the Chorus in the *Antigone*; but, unlike Bowra, Hogan suggests this is an unusual rather than a usual practice with Sophocles (*Commentary*, p. 135).

7. On divine law as basis for human law in ancient Greece, see Walter Burkest, *Greek Religion* (1985), pp. 247, 252; W. K. C. Guthrie, *The Sophists* (1971), p. 54.

8. Paolucci, *Hegel on Tragedy*, p. 325.

9. Ibid., pp. 48, 89, 178, 325.

10. On this point, see A. C. Bradley's "Hegel's Theory of Tragedy," appendix in *Hegel on Tragedy*, ed. Paolucci, pp. 370–71.

11. Paolucci, *Hegel on Tragedy*, p. 68.

12. For Hegel, a philosophical monist, ultimate reality is a single, organic, and dynamic whole. God, for Hegel, is Absolute Spirit coming to self-consciousness, through human consciousness, in history. Though Hegel's Absolute Spirit knows itself primarily through philosophy, yet art—supremely, Greek tragedy—also plays a role in this dynamic process.

13. George Steiner, *Antigones: The Antigone Myth in Western Literature, Art, and Thought* (1986), pp. 227, 262. Page numbers of further references to *Antigones* will be found in the text in parentheses after each citation.

14. On Aristotle's conception of unwritten law in the *Antigone*, see Hogan, *Commentary*, p. 144.

15. Ann Loades offers an alternative approach to Weil's interpretation of *Antigone* vis à vis George Steiner's *Antigones*. Loades endeavors to place Simone Weil within

the context of Steiner's book, as a whole, rather than opposing Steiner's own interpretation of the play to Weil's, as I have done ("Simone Weil and Antigone: Innocence and Affliction," in *Simone Weil's Philosophy of Culture: Readings toward a Divine Humanity* (1993), pp. 277–94).

16. Nussbaum, *Fragility of Goodness*, p. 52. Page numbers of further references to *Fragility of Goodness* will be found in parentheses after each citation.

17. On this point, see Guthrie, *The Sophists*, p. 54.

18. In 1936, two years before she became inspired by the Christian mysteries, Simone Weil wrote a summary of the *Antigone* for a workers' periodical (IC, 18–23). Her hope was to make a series of ancient Greek poems available to the average laborers on the grounds that these poems, however ancient, could better be understood by those who struggle and suffer than by those who spend their lives safely behind library walls. Unlike in later years, when Weil brings a sapiential perspective to her reading of the *Antigone*, Weil offers no spiritual interpretation of *Antigone* in her early comments. She does, however, perceive a moral tone in the play, for she views it as a play about good and evil. She holds up Antigone herself as a heroine who she believes is typically Sophoclean, a person noble and courageous who never lets herself be corrupted by misfortune, even at breaking point. This courage furnishes, Weil believes, the essential serenity of the play despite its unhappy outcome. In this summary, Weil views Creon's point of view as that of one who upholds the authority of the state. She does not, however, yet characterize Antigone's outlook as being specifically religious in opposition to Creon's secular orientation. Weil says more broadly of Antigone here, "She holds to another view which seems to her to be superior" (*IC*, 21).

Later on in this same early account of the play, Weil says that Creon sees in Haemon's criticisms of his treatment of Antigone only a threat to his own authority (210). Creon's discussion with the prophet Teiresias Weil describes as long and violent (23). Finally, Weil acknowledges the final choral statement as conclusive, pointing out that in the example of Creon we see punishment falling upon pride (23). Thus, Weil implicitly acknowledges Creon is not, as Hegel proposes, a moral force but rather someone who commits evil from pride and suffers therefore, even as his innocent victim does. Antigone herself is, at this point, for Weil, pure, innocent, heroic with a loving heart (20), unlike her sister Ismene, who is a shy sweet girl such as those one encounters every day (20). For Weil, Antigone therefore is not partially right but partially wrong and therefore narrow, as the Hegelian has it, but heroic to the core, as the classic Sophoclean critic views her.

During or before the same period in which she wrote a series of articles for the French workers, Weil wrote in her notebooks that, though the Sophoclean hero is shattered by a hostile destiny, this character always retains human form (*FLN*, 33). Though *Antigone*, specifically, is a drama of loneliness—a loneliness which includes the appearance of guilt, abandonment, weakness (*FLN*, 32–33)—yet, Weil suggests, Sophocles shows that through all adversity nothing can destroy inner freedom (*FLN*, 49).

In Weil's early talk of *Antigone*, particularly in the characterization of Antigone herself, there is, then, the belief that a paramount ideal exists for Sophocles, an ideal moral in kind. The significance of Sophocles' tragedies lies in his characters' ability to maintain this ideal through even the harshest realities of life. Already, then, these early comments place Weil closer to the classic Sophoclean rather than the Hegelian interpreters of the *Antigone*.

19. Schuon, *Transcendent Unity of Religions*, pp. 53, 56.

20. See n. 18, above.

21. Steiner, *Antigones*, p. 282.

22. Nussbaum, *Fragility of Goodness*, p. 66.

23. Bernard Knox, *The Heroic Temper: Studies in Sophoclean Tragedy* (1964), pp. 103, 107.

24. *Antigone*, lines 898–99. (On this passage, see Bowra, *Sophoclean Tragedy*, p. 104).

25. The final lines of the *kommos* (Antigone's last lines in the play) bear sufficient witness to the unwavering quality of Antigone's reverence for the gods, as to her refusal to disown the act of burying her brother even despite the death sentence it brings her: "O city of Thebes where my fathers dwelt, / O gods of our race...How savagely impious men use me, / For keeping a law that is holy" (910–916).

26. The following critics offer support for Weil's belief that Antigone's will and the divine will harmonize: Bowra, *Sophoclean Tragedy*, p. 88; Hogan, *Commentary*, p. 144; Ehrenberg, *Sophocles and Pericles*, p. 57; Reinhardt, *Sophocles*, p. 77.

27. William Shakespeare, *The Tragedy of King Lear* in *The Riverside Shakespeare* (1974), V.iii.8–18. Further references to *King Lear* are to this edition and will be cited in the text.

28. This debate itself is fully articulated in ch. 1 of William R. Elton's *"King Lear" and the Gods* (1988). Page numbers of further references to *"King Lear" and the Gods* will be found in parentheses after each citation.

29. Bradley, *Shakespearean Tragedy*, p. 253.

30. Stephen Booth, *King Lear, Macbeth, Indefinition, and Tragedy* (1983), pp. 21–22; Robert Hunter, *Shakespeare and the Mystery of God's Judgments* (1976), p. 196; Nicholas Brooke, "On Moral Structure vs. Experience," in *Twentieth Century Interpretations of King Lear* (1978), p. 127.

31. This core concern is clearly enough stated in Shakespeare's source, *The Chronicle History of King Leir: The Original of Shakespeare's 'King Lear'* (1909), p. 71.

32. Roy Battenhouse, *Shakespearean Tragedy: Its Art and Its Christian Premises* (1969), p. 292. Page numbers of further references to *Shakespearean Tragedy* will be found in parentheses after each citation.

33. In a note on p. 442, Battenhouse qualifies significantly his supernatural interpretation of the play's end.

34. Martin Lings, *The Secret of Shakespeare* (1984), p. 76. Page numbers of further references to *The Secret of Shakespeare* will be found in parentheses after each citation.

35. In her "Letter to an Oxford Poet" (L, 103–4), Weil cites the six passages from *King Lear* as follows:

> ...Life and Death! I am ashamed
> That thou hast power to shake my manhood thus;
> That these hot tears, which break from me perforce,
> Should make thee worth them...[I.iv.296–99]
>
> O let me not be mad, not mad, sweet heaven!
> Keep me in temper: I would not be mad! [I.v.46–47]
>
> You heavens, give me that patience, patience I need!
> You see me here, you gods, a poor old man,
> As full of grief as age; wretched in both:
> If it be you that stirs these daughters' hearts
> Against their father, fool me not so much
> To bear it tamely; touch me with noble anger,
> And let not women's weapons, water-drops,
> Stain my man's cheeks!...[II.iv.271–78]
>
> ...You think I'll weep;
> No, I'll not weep:
> I have full cause of weeping; but this heart
> Shall break into a hundred thousand flaws
> Or ere I'll weep, O fool, I shall go mad! [II.iv.282–86]
>
> ...O Regan, Goneril!
> Your kind old father, whose frank heart gave you all—
> O, that way madness lies; let me shun that;
> No more of that. [III.iv.19–22]
>
> Why should a dog, a horse, a rat have life,
> And thou no breath at all? [V.iii.307–8]

Chapter Four

Tragedy of Crime and the Sacred: *Oedipus Rex* and *Phèdre*

Tragedy of crime, like tragedy of calamity, evokes religious mystery, a suprarational ideal, an absolute good that includes but also transcends moral law. The suffering through which an absolute good reveals itself in this second type of tragedy, however, is moral in kind. A student of moral tragedy such as Martha Nussbaum offers the fact of compulsory wrongdoing, in literature and in life, as an irrefutable witness against the existence of any supernatural good that might be said to reign supreme in a tragic world.[1] A Weilian approach to moral tragedy opposes this influential modernist view. The mystery of Christ's cross contains not only suffering innocence but tragic or guiltless guilt as well.

Like Martin Luther, first theologian of the cross, Simone Weil points out in her time the loss of the sense of degradation and the infamy of Christ's passion (*IC*, 142). She laments a lack of the feeling that he has been made sin and a curse for humankind (*NB*, 204; *SNL*, 173). She regrets, thus, a weakened sense of the Christ's truly having taken upon himself the sins of the world and of his having felt rejected not only by men but also by God. Persons have forgotten that even the Christ, for a time, lost the sense of his own righteousness.

For Luther, when Christ was made to become sin, the greatest transgressor of all, the sins of the world became "Christ's own sins as really as if he himself had done them";

there can, he believes, be no knowledge of Christ without this knowledge.[2]

A contemplation of Sophocles' *Oedipus Rex* and Racine's *Phèdre* by the light of Christ's cross reveals the error of those many students of Christian tragedy who believe that guiltless guilt or compulsory wrongdoing can find no place in a Christian outlook.[3]

Like Antigone and King Lear, so Oedipus and Phèdre also spiritually transcend the humiliation of affliction, but in their cases affliction makes itself felt not as a suffering technically innocent (or nearly so) but rather as a compulsion to commit actual crime. By placing their trust in a good beyond reason, a good that includes though it transcends moral law, both characters experience a painful catharsis of soul. According to Christian belief, though technically innocent, the crucified Christ himself suffers guilt in all its degradation and infamy. Christ's perfect love for the Father, occurring at the moment of dereliction, transcends not only innocent pain but the humiliation and self-contempt of the scapegoat as well. An understanding of Christ's suffering of love on the cross must include an experience of all the accursedness that accompanies crime. Thus, a story of guiltless guilt, no less than a tale of suffering innocence, may evoke the cross. A tragedy of crime, no less than a tragedy of calamity, may mysteriously justify the order of the world.

Oedipus Rex

Those modernist critics who question the piety of Sophocles' plays find in the *Oedipus Rex* an incontrovertibly clear example of Sophoclean skepticism, a questioning of the divine beneficence. The *Oedipus Rex* describes the horrifying plight of a man who, against his will—indeed, in complete ignorance—kills his own father and marries his mother. These crimes remain unknown to Oedipus until they are publicly revealed, ironically, through Oedipus' own efforts, at the height of the king's power and popularity. The very story itself may be said to pose a challenge to theodicy deeper even than a play like the *Antigone* or *King Lear*, for here the challenge to the divine justice is a hero who does not simply suffer innocently but who commits grievous sins against his will, according to divine prediction or plan.

I will refer to three sections in particular in the analysis of this play. The opening lines of the second stasimon—a choral ode in praise of divine law—constitutes the first of the three significant parts. The chorus recites this ode at a time in the play when Oedipus' wife, Jocasta, and Oedipus himself question the oracles of Apollo. They doubt both the prediction that Laius, former king of Thebes, would be slain by his son, as that Oedipus would slay his father and marry his mother. The ode begins as follows:

> CHORUS: I pray that I may pass my life
> In reverent holiness of word and deed.
> For there are laws enthroned above;
> Heaven created them,
> Olympus was their father,
> And mortal men had no part in their birth;
> Nor ever shall their power pass from sight
> In dull forgetfulness;
> A god moves in them; he grows not old.[4]

The second passage contains Oedipus' defense of his self-blinding. These lines occur in the latter part of the play. Oedipus perpetrates the self-mutilation when he discovers that he is the slayer of Laius, his father, and that Jocasta, Laius' wife, is his mother. (By this point in the play, Jocasta has committed suicide.) Oedipus' self-knowledge comes about as a result of his own efforts as king to rid Thebes of a plague which had smitten the town. The plague had arisen from a moral pollution caused by the unknown slayer of Laius, the city's former king. At the time of the play's opening, the killer had not yet been found or, therefore, brought to justice. After he puts out his eyes, in horror of his own guilt, Oedipus explains to the Chorus why he blinded rather than killed himself:

That what is done was not done for the best
Seek not to teach me: counsel me no more.
I know not how I could have gone to Hades
And with these eyes have looked upon my father
Or on my mother; such things have I done
To them, death is no worthy punishment.
Or could I look for pleasure in the sight
Of my own children, born as they were born?
Never! No pleasure there, for eyes of mine,
Nor in this city, nor its battlements
Nor sacred images. From these—ah, miserable!—
I, the most nobly born of any Theban
Am banned for ever by my own decree
That the defiler should be driven forth,
The man accursed of Heaven and Laius' house.
....
...Quick as you can, I beg,
Banish me, hide me....Throw me forth
Into the sea, where I may sink from view.
I pray you, deign to touch one so afflicted,
And do not fear: there is no man alive
Can bear this load of evil but myself. (1308–54)

The third significant passage is the concluding dialogue of the play. These are Oedipus' final words, occurring in a conversation with Creon, his brother-in-law:

OEDIPUS: You know what I would have you do?
CREON: If you will tell me, I shall know.
OEDIPUS: Send me away, away from Thebes.
CREON: The God, not I, must grant you this.
OEDIPUS: The gods hate no man more than me!
CREON: Then what you ask they soon will give.
OEDIPUS: You promise this?
CREON: Ah, no! When I
Am ignorant, I do not speak.
OEDIPUS: Then lead me in; I say no more.
CREON: Release the children then, and come.
OEDIPUS: What? Take these children from me? No!

CREON: Seek not to have your way in all things:
Where you had your way before,
Your mastery broke before the end. (1451–64)

The issue that lies at the deepest point of debate concerning the pious quality of the *Oedipus Rex* is the nature of Oedipus' relationship to the gods. The modernist, though he often takes the gods into account and acknowledges their importance in the play, tends to neglect to take seriously the idea of relationship between the human and the divine.[5] In this the modernist's tendency to sidestep the moral issue at the heart of the play is especially telling, for as in any authentically religious outlook—a worldview, I propose, the *Oedipus Rex* itself manifests—it is precisely in the matter of good and evil that man finds his meeting ground with the divine. And nowhere else.

I will discuss the issue of man's relationship with the divine in *Oedipus Rex* as C. M. Bowra and Bernard Knox, respectively, view it. As in our discussion of the *Antigone*, I will again offer Bowra as an example of a "classic" Sophoclean critic, one who retains Sophocles' own religious views. Knox, one of many modernist commentators, holds to a more experimental, amoral point of view. Simone Weil herself, we shall see, harmonizes a classic with a Christian esoteric reading of this play.

For both Bowra and Knox, Oedipus is a great man. The former, classic critic discovers the king's greatness in a profound capacity for a spirit of reverence, for a sense of modesty before the gods. This greatness is not fully revealed until the end of the play, for it is a virtue whose actualization Oedipus' social success impedes. Oedipus' humble reverence for the divine itself implies the possibility of a relationship between the divine and the human. This harmonization is possible only on moral grounds. This ground is furnished by the existence of sacred moral law. On the other hand, Knox, a modernist critic, believes Oedipus' greatness lies not in a spirit of reverence but rather in a defiant pride that never changes, even in the severest adversities. Oedipus' heroism consists in resisting, rather than in coming into harmony with, the divine.

The distinction between rational culpability and a more mysterious, more general sense of moral failure, experienced by Oedipus as a pollution, constitutes a central issue in discussions concerning the relationship between Oedipus and the gods. Bowra, for example, derives from Oedipus' mysterious moral degradation Sophocles' central statement regarding the relationship between man and the gods. This relationship hinges on the existence of a moral law which is sanctioned by the divine. Knox, on the other hand, detaches Oedipus from his crimes and their attendant pollution. This critic views the role of the divine in the play as one of divine prescience or foreknowledge only.[6] From a classic perspective, by excluding the gods' province over unwritten law, Knox excludes the only point of possible contact between man and god—the matter of good and evil.

Knox de-moralizes the purport of the second stasimon, the lines praising unwritten law. He posits that the Chorus refers in this ode to Oedipus as a symbol of Athens. Both Oedipus and Athens are doomed, despite their greatness, to pointless calamity (100–6). Bowra, on the other hand, suggests the second stasimon emphasizes the divine underpinning of all human morality.[7] The ode connects the rises and falls of human fortune to the breaking or keeping of sacred laws. The mutability of human life always carries moral purport.

Knox suggests that good and evil can not be said to be a central issue in the *Oedipus Rex*, because Oedipus is not in a rational sense guilty of a moral fault: Oedipus commits both parricide and incest unwittingly (49). Indeed, for Knox, it is not a moral flaw but rather Oedipus' energy and his intelligence that bring about his downfall.

Knox offers persuasive evidence that vigor, intelligence, and self-confidence manifest themselves in Oedipus' search for the killer of Laius. These are positive qualities which meet inevitable defeat in a world ruled by what Knox regards as irrational rather than suprarational powers. From the perspective of a classic Sophoclean critic, however, Knox's conception of Oedipus as heroic victim of amoral forces takes out of account the central emotion of the play: the feeling of guilt. The classic critic will point out that, in his piety, and even before he knows the truth for sure, Oedipus abhors the simple idea that he himself could be guilty of such a crime as murder (much less parricide and incest).[8] Comparably, in a classic vein, Oedipus' dominating obsession after the discovery of his criminal acts is the feeling of being accursed. Though his acts were unwitting, Oedipus himself feels polluted by the most abominable sins a human being can commit. Oedipus' deepest torment is his conviction that he is despised by the gods, as loathed of men. Contrary to a classic interpretation, Knox, a modernist, regards Oedipus as heroic victim of an order of things which dooms him without cause or moral purport. For Knox, therefore, Oedipus' guilt and shame are essentially irrelevant.

Some critics, classic and modernist alike, downplay or ignore the last fifth of the play, the section following Oedipus' complete awakening regarding his crimes.[9] Knox, however, devotes a whole chapter of his book-length study to this portion of the play; yet, from a classic perspective, Knox makes puzzlingly scant reference to Oedipus' humiliation, his overwhelming sense of shame, his degradation. According to Knox, after Oedipus discovers he has unwittingly committed parricide and incest, the Greek king, ever versatile, quickly adapts to his new "role" and becomes "irresistible" as a beggar (191). The self-blinding, Bowra points out, Oedipus himself explains as a gesture of shame—for how dead in the underworld rather than alive and blind can he look upon mother and father? (183). Knox, contrarily, views the self-blinding as a sign that the self-asserting king of the outset of the play, determined to do all he can to save his city from plague and then to discover his own identity, has triumphantly returned (186). Even in the lines just following the self-blinding—the passage where Oedipus asks to be taken, hidden, thrown quickly away from mortal sight—Knox takes no note of the take, the hide, the throw, verbs that reveal Oedipus' self-contempt. Knox comments, rather, on the "quickly," the word that modifies these verbs. Knox uses this adverb as an indication that Oedipus, rather than humiliated, weighed down with self-contempt and guilt, is ever assertive, a man of action (188). Yet, Bowra indicates, these verbs are the very words which end the beautiful, horrifying, heart-rending passage in which Oedipus describes himself as a scapegoat, a polluted being whose suffering and exile alone can purify the city he has himself long led in pride and glory (183). From Bowra's perspective, all this speech is uttered in explanation of Oedipus' self-blinding. The act of maiming itself bears witness not to an indomitable self-assertion (as Knox maintains) but to the infinite weight of degradation upon him, degradation as he feels before father, mother, children, city, the gods—indeed, all that lives and breathes (183).

Soon after Oedipus utters the speech in which he defends his self-mutilation to the Chorus—the second passage cited above—Creon reminds Oedipus that the source of light itself, the sun, must not be defiled by the sight of him (Sophocles, 1361–70). Initially, Oedipus prefers to be exiled rather than taken within the palace, where Creon would have him hidden from the sun. At play's end, however, in an act of perfect heart-rending self-denial, Oedipus assents to Creon's wish that Oedipus be led inside, out of the light of day. The third passage above describes this consent. According to a classic view, Oedipus indicates by his obedience to Creon that he accepts his destiny. In agreement with Creon, Oedipus is willing to work with the god to see that he makes amends for his crimes. He will make his amends not as he, but as the god himself, wills. For this, Bowra asserts, the ancient Greeks could only admire him (172, 185). Contrary to a classic reading, Knox characterizes Oedipus at the very close of the play as the reconstituted hero of the opening scene—imperious and dynamic (185). Knox's Oedipus is self-asserting to the last.

Knox interprets the rule by the gods which is vindicated by the veracity of Apollo's' predictions as a victory for "mischance." Here, at the end of his chapter on the role of the divine, Knox identifies mischance with divine chance. Yet, earlier in the chapter, Knox defines "divine chance" as something subordinate, in the traditional ancient religions, to other gods and therefore associated with, and not opposed to, order, as chance would otherwise be. Thus, at the conclusion of his discussion, Knox interprets "divine chance" not as he earlier describes it, as subordinate to the other gods, but as equivalent to an irrational force or "mischance" (181).

Knox, then, though with some inconsistency, regards the gods in *Oedipus Rex* as irrational forces unconcerned with the welfare of heroic man. He offers no reference to the gods' role in the play as guardians of moral law. Bowra, on the other hand, perceives Oedipus' violation of moral law, however unwitting, as a problem central to the play. Yet despite Bowra's insistence on the important place of good and evil, Bowra acknowledges the complexity of the moral issues at stake in the play. Indeed, in agreement with critics such as Knox, Bowra suggests that, in rational or legal terms, Oedipus is innocent not only by modern but also by ancient Greek standards (165). Concomitantly, Bowra points out that Oedipus' suffering can not legitimately be viewed as a function of divine punishment, either as a result of *hamartia* or pride or an inherited curse (162ff.). However, Bowra departs from a modernist critic such as Knox when he suggests that the play dramatizes not its protagonist's proud, self-assertive heroism but rather the crisis that humbles Oedipus, revealing him as polluted. The play also shows the steps Oedipus takes to overcome the gulf between himself and the gods caused by this pollution. For Bowra, this is what the play is about (176–7). Further, the greatest obstacle between Oedipus and the truth is the sense of his own importance. Paradoxically, by losing his self-importance, Oedipus becomes a greater man at the end of the play, revealed as ignorant and polluted, than at the beginning when he is an honored king famed for his intelligence and his goodness alike (210). From Bowra's perspective, it is wrong to say, as Knox does (49), that the only fault at issue in the play is an intellectual and not a moral fault. Thus, an amoral interpretation need not be the only alternative to a rational, moralistic one.

As we have already seen in his assessment of the *Antigone*, Bowra believes that the Sophoclean gods are not an irrational force, as Knox regards them. The gods, who know everything, are right. "Nor may man complain of them. He must humble himself before them and admit that he is nothing and that he knows nothing. This is the lesson of King Oedipus" (209). Bowra suggests that in modern terms the gods appear cruel but that Sophocles would likely ascribe such impressions to human ignorance (378). By this, Bowra implies that Sophocles speaks of suprarational rather than irrational forces. Indeed, according to Bowra, suffering constitutes not a punishment for Oedipus but the occasion for a salutary lesson (377). Unlike Aristotle's superficial, essentially secular, idea of discovery in Greek tragedy, still following Bowra, Sophocles' concept of discovery concerns nothing less than man's discovery of his status in the eyes of the gods: Man doesn't know himself until he knows how he stands with the gods (365). All else is unimportant by comparison. Thus, the intellectual ingenuity of an Oedipus who alone solved the riddle of the sphinx and thereby saved the people of Thebes from the beast's power—this intellectual, this moral superiority, are nought so long as Oedipus' peace has not been made with the divine.

As we have seen, according to Bowra, Oedipus sees himself as a polluted being whose expulsion will purify the city (183). When Oedipus discovers that he himself is the murderer of Laius, out of reverence for the divine will, he carries out upon himself the curse he, as king, had called down on the murderer. From the outset of the play, at the time of Apollo's call for purification, to its very end, when Oedipus accepts his position as the polluted one, Oedipus displays a spirit of reverence for the divine (172). From a classic perspective, then, a modernist such as Knox can make nothing of Oedipus' humiliation in the play's final scene, because he makes nothing of the divine laws in honor of which the curse was uttered.

The temporary skepticism of Jocasta and Oedipus, then, are proved wrong at the last (Bowra, 191, 198, 297–98). Apollo's oracles only *appear* to have been thwarted. In the end both of the oracles are seen to have been fulfilled. In this play, even as in the *Antigone*, despite the suspense, the word and the will of the gods are vindicated at the last.

It is true that, as Knox points out, *Oedipus Rex* affirms divine prescience but, as Bowra suggests, the sacredness of moral law also is highlighted. The holiness of moral relations is upheld through the only means possible: the existence and the reliability of the divine (205). Thus the faith in divine law which the Chorus expresses in the second stasimon is not disappointed. From a classic perspective, then, not "mischance," an irrational force, but the gods, suprarational beings, lie at the root of the play's action. This is a world where order reigns. Though it is an order that does not preclude pain, it is foolish as well as impious not to accept as to revere it.[10]

Simone Weil, who shares the classic critic's reading of Sophocles, reveals that there exists a Christian tone in the harsh melody of the *Oedipus Rex*, no less than in the discordant song of the *Antigone*. This heart-rending but harmonious strain may be said, from a Christian perspective, to furnish a theodicy of mystery to the play.

Though Weil maintains at one point that all the heroes of Sophocles are noble heroes, never allowing themselves to be corrupted by misfortune (*IC*, 19), yet she acknowledges specifically the impurity of Oedipus. She speaks of Oedipus as the son of disobedience (referring apparently to Laius' original disobedience of an oracle), truly defiled, through incest. In this, Weil contrasts Oedipus with Antigone and Eteocles, whom she regards as pure rather than impure victims, pure because obedient unto death (*NB*, 561). Weil regards Oedipus as sinful, then, but unwittingly, as a result of an inherited curse (*NB*, 560–61). Thus, contrary to modernists, Weil views Oedipus' pollution as being something central to his story.

Further, when Weil speaks of *Oedipus Rex* and *Oedipus at Colonus*, with common reference to the *Antigone*, she refers to the utter abandonment of the protagonists, the aloneness of the heroes, their beggary and appearance of guilt. She describes these protagonists' total and sudden loss of wealth, power, and honor as a result of pure chance. She speaks also of privations, the humiliation of supplication, the feeling of abandonment, the brutality of nature

(*FLN*, 32–33). Weil notes that Sophocles' dramas generally reveal the vulnerability and loneliness of the individual. She simultaneously asserts that the Sophoclean protagonists are energetic as a rule. Like Bowra, however, she admits sheer human vitality as a secondary, rather than primary, quality (*FLN*, 32–33).

Weil, then, emphasizes the human weakness rather than the defiant strength of the Sophoclean hero. The greatness of Sophocles' heroes lies not in pride or intelligence or energy but in a quiet heart-breaking nobility: the refusal to be corrupted even amid the sorest trials. Sophocles' heroes boast a moral preeminence which, in later writings, Weil regards as being supramoral in character. Indeed, Weil's own unfinished tragedy, *Venise Sauvée*, attempts to revive the supernatural nobility Weil believes characterizes the Sophoclean hero.[11]

The above references to *Oedipus Rex* place Weil within the camp of classic rather than modernist interpreters. Three further passages must be looked to, however, if a Weilian interpretation may be offered for the quotations from *Oedipus Rex* cited at the outset of this discussion: the passages concerning unwritten law, the king's self-blinding, and Oedipus' final acquiescence to Creon. Together these three sections from Weil's works will reveal the theodicy of mystery at the heart of this shocking play.

1. In her notebooks, following a discussion of miracles, Weil asserts that the theater and art have the ability to point to the existence of a "third dimension" in the world. Weil lists specifically the *Oedipus Rex* as an example of a drama with this capability (*NB*, 244).

Apparently, the presence of the third dimension in the world constitutes earthly contact with the supernatural. Weil believes the presence of the supernatural in life is something infinitely small but decisive (*OL*, 166). This decisive quality is made possible by the wise persuasion through which, in Plato's *Timaeus*, God moves those things necessary, things indifferent to the good, toward the Good (*OL*, 166). As we have seen, this wise persuasion at the time of the creation Weil regards as being the crucified Christ. A human being may assimilate himself to a supernatural Good by imitating the unconditional consent of the Christ to the order of the world established at the time of the creation. Sacred art, for Weil, constitutes an imitation of this assimilation. Apparently Weil believed *Oedipus Rex*, then, describes a human soul who, like the crucified one, continues to maintain an attitude of love for the good even in extreme affliction.

2. The following comment provides a second basis for discovering a theodicy of mystery in *Oedipus Rex*. These lines concern Sophocles' idea of unwritten law:

"One is nearer the sky at the top of the mountain than in the plain. But one is no nearer to flying. One is exactly as far away as before.

"That is why pride is a mistake. When we fly if we are really flying we have come out of ourself, and there is no more pride.

"The good begins at a point beyond the reach of will, as truth begins at a point beyond the reach of intelligence. Beyond the intelligence, and therefore beyond the law. The true law is an unwritten law, as Sophocles knew. For the letter kills" (*FLN*, 262).

According to this passage, the true good is a function not of the human being's relationship with his fellows or with law in any rational sense; rather, it is a function of his direct relationship with the divine. The true good, one which reaches beyond the intelligence and therefore beyond the rational, is humility. The true good, then, is something that reaches beyond moral character. In this sense Oedipus himself may be said to "fly." Oedipus comes out of himself utterly, including out of his own moral character, when he accepts the fate of compulsory wrongdoing in a spirit of reverence. The true good, humility, constitutes obedience, but this is an obedience suprarational rather than rational in kind.

3. Simone Weil's concept of nontangible or psychic matter, derived from the work of Karl Marx, illuminates further how not simply suffering innocence but even compulsory wrongdoing may be regarded as a part of a just world.

"Among all the forms of materialism, the work of Marx contains one extremely valuable indication," Weil asserts, "although he himself made hardly any real use of it...the idea of non-physical matter. Marx...directed his attention only to social matter....When we think of matter, we think of a mechanical system of forces subject to a blind and rigorous necessity. The same applies to that non-tangible matter which is the substance of our thoughts" (*OL*, 178). Weil proceeds to point out, in the spirit of such modern students of moral tragedy as Stanley Hauerwas and Martha Nussbaum,[12] that moral phenomena are not arbitrary and cannot, therefore, always be brought about by an act of will (178). The contrary idea that the human being is always master of his or her moral behavior is an erroneous belief which, for Weil, the Marxian concept of nontangible matter could help to eradicate.

In a later section of the passage quoted above, Weil supports her belief that moral tragedy or compulsory wrong-doing is a real possibility in human life. She offers two examples of human behavior which she suggests an onlooker, and even the doer himself, would be likely to condemn. Weil explains that there are at work in these instances, as in many human actions, certain nontangible stimuli which the human person cannot control. Such stimuli are the function of a realm of matter indifferent to the good. They make certain behavior, however desirable, impossible.

Martha Nussbaum and Stanley Hauerwas contemplate the phenomenon of moral tragedy outside the context of the concomitant problem of theodicy. Weil's theory of creation through the cross, a kenotic or self-emptying act, enables Weil, however, to accept even the existence of necessary moral evil as something which comes from a good God. When God surrendered himself in the act of creation, He surrendered himself not only to a blind necessity but also to the faculty of free consent within souls (*WG*, 158). This latter faculty is always immune to the rule of matter, including nontangible matter. For Weil, it is in the willingness or unwillingness freely to surrender this consent, even irrespective of the human being's ability or inability to keep to a sacred moral code, that the human being's relationship with God ultimately consists. Thus, according to Weil's metaphysics, it is possible to believe that a person may remain essentially good even while performing an act that violates moral law and also that a good God is the author of a world order where such things are possible. In such a world, the supreme human virtue, then, becomes humility or supernatural obedience rather than righteousness. The supreme human good is unconditioned reverence for the divine will.

Thus, Weil's thoughts on the suprarational import of Sophocles' plays in general (unwritten law), and on *Oedipus Rex* in particular (the third dimension), find completion in her conception of compulsory wrongdoing (nontangible matter).

In Weilian terms, then, although he is not only a successful king but also a good king, at the outset of the play, Oedipus still falls short of perfection. Like all human beings, he prides himself on his accomplishments, including his moral ones. He is insufficiently aware of his dependence on a force exterior to himself for all things. Above all, he is insufficiently aware of the divine source, the sacred quality of the moral laws which he prides himself on keeping. As Weil says, man needs to think of himself as a limited and dependent creature; only suffering can teach him this (*IC*, 57). Without understanding his own limitations, particularly his moral limitations, man cannot know God, nor, paradoxically, can he be genuinely good.

Thus Weil, like Bowra, offers a basis for interpreting the choral ode on unwritten law as being of central importance to Oedipus' story. The opening of this ode praises the divine source of moral law. No less important, from a Weilian perspective, is the passage describing Oedipus' feeling of accursedness when he discovers his pollution, his unwitting violation of divine law. This feeling of moral degradation causes Oedipus to blind himself. The passage bears witness to the kind of humiliation that only contact with evil, violation of the sacred, can bring. Finally, Oedipus' willingness to make amends for a sin he did not willfully commit, a desire manifested in his final dialogue with Creon, exhibits a fundamental love of the good which triumphs over even unmerited infamy and degradation. Thus, perfect in his modesty before the divine at the close of the play, according to a Weilian reading, Oedipus is, indeed, as Bowra suggests, a better man at the end of the play, humiliated and polluted, than at its start, proud and self-confident.

Weil asserts that, in a certain sense, it is better to sin than to take oneself seriously (*NB*, 141). In this respect, indeed, she sees sinning as a favorable circumstance (*NB*, 249). Only if we do as the Greeks did, only if we love God through our sin (Weil may well have had Oedipus in mind), is it God and not some projection or image of ourselves, such as our own moral character, that we love (*NB*, 88). Only thus do we learn that love of God is an unconditional feeling, independent of our crimes as well as our misfortunes (*FLN*, 199). The penal quality of one's suffering, then, is important, for it robs the human person of all prestige (*IC*, 137) and therefore all self-importance. Christ is close to the criminals for these reasons (*LGA*, 176, 194). Humility is the only way to be like God (*FLN*, 296–97), as revealed by the crucified Christ, whose own guilt was guiltless and whose moral perfection consisted in his unconditional trust in the divine will. This obedience is equivalent to a love for the good which is not crushed even by the iron hand of self-denigration.

Oedipus violates the sacred when he commits parricide and incest, even though unconscious of his crimes at the time he committed them. Oedipus not only violates the sacred, however. He affirms the sacred as well when, out of humility, an obedience which transcends the legalistic or rational, he assumes responsibility for his acts of wrongdoing, even though they were not conscious acts. This assumption of responsibility constitutes the suprarational consent to obey the divine will, one which accepts the necessary not in the form of innocent suffering but rather as compulsory wrongdoing. Only something suprarational could impel Oedipus to assume responsibility for crimes that were not deliberate, not consciously chosen. Humility before a power greater than human alone, a suprarational power, one which undergirds moral law, could alone impel one who has violated moral law unwittingly to repent simultaneously that violation.

For Weil, supernatural obedience, the mystic's *fiat voluntas tua* (your will be done), is the only pure motive in the spiritual life because it alone holds no reward for one's own action in view (*GG*, 97). Thus, no less than the technically innocent Antigone, even Oedipus, the polluted, the degraded one, achieves a state of catharsis or spiritual purification to the point of perfection. This moment occurs, as we have indicated, when Oedipus, heart-breakingly, assents to Creon's wish that he be removed to the palace from the light of day, there to attend knowledge of the gods' will. At this moment, perhaps the most extreme moment of his affliction, rather than seeking solace in an attitude of anger or bitterness, Oedipus sustains an attitude of quiet, heart-breaking love for what is good.

As we have seen, for Weil, the creation bears the stamp of Christ's cross. Sacred art reveals the cruciform character of the world. The cross itself constitutes a supreme instance of innocent suffering, yet as a crucifixion, the cross of Christ comprises a suffering of degradation and infamy at the same time. The sinful suffering, like the innocent anguish, is transcended through Christ's perfect love for the Father even at the moment when Christ believes the Father has rejected him. This rejection is felt in its degrading aspect as an abandonment to the sins of the world. In this sense, the cross may be said to become a paradigm of tragic, or guiltless, guilt. A story like Oedipus' can help us to attend the sordid fate Christ gently suffered on the cross, an infamy endured against his will yet at the same time consented to. The *Oedipus Rex* may offer a means of contemplating Christ's cross; however, the possibility of this meditation may be actuated only if the Oedipus story is not gutted, as modernist critics, in particular, prune *Oedipus Rex*, of the emotional horrors, the hell of guilt, the anguish of infamy, that Oedipus heart-breakingly and patiently endures.

Oedipus thus manifests a love for the good even when he finds himself personally deprived of that good, not only rejected by men but apparently abandoned by the gods as well. Only such a love for the good, a mad love which persists even when a person finds himself lost in the belly of evil, will make a heart cry out without ceasing, even as the golden-hearted Oedipus cries out from the moment of his awakening concerning his sins until the end of the play, "My God, my God, why have you abandoned me?" Yet, in the manner of the crucified Christ, Oedipus sustains a love for the good even in moral despair.

So we may argue that Oedipus, no less than Antigone, by consenting to accept the world's order in all its blindness and cruelty, in a spirit of humble obedience, acknowledges as absolute the very essence of the order itself. This is a divine order. It is the source of the sacred or irrefragable quality of all human bonds.[13]

A Weilian viewpoint, however, would deepen Sophocles' injunction to respect or revere the world's order with an encouragement to love it as well, to love that world even to the point of madness, as Christ loved the author of the world even while nailed on a cross.

Thus a Weilian interpretation of *Oedipus Rex* holds the distinctions between good and evil at its core, as it gives pride of place to the matter of the sacred quality of divine or unwritten law. From a classic perspective, then, Weil's thoughts avoid the modernist tendency to see irrationality where suprarationality exists. Simultaneously, a Weilian interpretation points to an affinity between the classic Sophoclean vision and the Christian outlook in its esoteric dimension. The idea of compulsory wrongdoing, then, is not necessarily incompatible with a Christian outlook; nor is the supernatural, generally speaking, anti-tragic. Indeed, as Weil shows, the supernatural forms an essential part of tragic experience.

Phèdre

Although Racine, unlike Sophocles, lived in a Christian age, the putative religious nature of the last and greatest of Racine's "profane" plays has been much disputed, particularly in recent years. Racine's contemporary, the famous Jansenist, Antoine Arnauld, expressed moral and religious satisfaction with *Phèdre.*[14] In the moralizing preface to his play, Racine himself caters in part to Jansenist friends.[15] Still in our own century, in Jansenist fashion, Phèdre is described as a Christian woman to whom grace has been denied.[16] Yet, despite these facts, there exists among major twentieth-century critics of Racine strenuous and intelligent objection that *Phèdre* is not a Christian work, Jansenist or otherwise. To this objection Simone Weil's thoughts on the play bring illumination.

The *Oedipus Rex*, it has been proposed, directly inspired Racine's *Phèdre.*[17] If this is true, it is no surprise that the chief problem posed to a religious reading of *Phèdre* is the relationship the play delineates between the human and the divine. In this play a goddess, Venus, dooms Phèdre to an unconquerable incestuous and adulterous passion. Does such a play offer a world vision compatible with the Christian belief in an all-powerful God who is also good?

The passages of *Phèdre* which will form the basis for our discussion are two. The first constitutes Phèdre's deepest moment of despair. This is a time when Phèdre (like the polluted Oedipus) seeks to hide from all that lives. The moment of profoundest anguish comes in the fourth act. By this point in the play, through the encouragement of her nurse, Oenone, and as a result of the false news that her husband, Theseus, is dead, Phèdre has proclaimed her adulterous and incestuous passion to Hippolytus. Phèdre, rejected by her stepson with horror, hears subsequently that her husband is alive, despite the rumoring abroad to the contrary, and also that he has returned home. A hopeless slave of her passion, Phèdre passively allows Oenone to take action in her favor upon Theseus' return. Phèdre's nurse, thus, accuses Hippolytus of making illicit advances against Phèdre during Theseus' absence. Phèdre is prevented from confessing to Theseus the falseness of Oenone's charges only by news that Hippolytus loves the princess Aricie. It is the revelation that Hippolytus loves this woman that brings Phèdre to the deepest point of her affliction. In addition to the irrelevant but genuine jealousy aroused by knowledge of a rival, Phèdre cannot but compare the guilt of her own unconquerable passion for her stepson with the innocence of the love she has just discovered exists:

> All I have suffered, my fears, my ecstasies,
> frenzy of longing, horror of remorse,
> intolerable insult of rejection,
> were but a weak foreshadowing of this torment.
> ....
>   Alas,
> they saw each other with impunity.
> Heaven blessed their innocent desire, they followed
> the leaning of their hearts without remorse;
> day after day rose calm and clear for them.
> And I, sorrowful outcast from all nature,
> hid myself from the morning, fled the light.

And now, when she catches herself plotting the destruction of Aricie, counting on the help of her husband in order to accomplish her jealous revenge, Phèdre cries out for a hiding place. Where can she hide?

> What am I saying? Where will my reason wander?
> I, jealous! And it is Theseus I implore!
> ....
>   Now and henceforth
> my crimes have reached to the full brimming measure.
> I breathe, at the same moment, guile and incest.
> My life-destroying hands, quick for revenge,
> are burning to be plunged in innocent blood.
> Miserable! And I live, and can bear the eye
> of that holy Sun from whom I am descended?
> My grandfather is master of the Gods;
> my ancestors crowd heaven, the universe.
> Where hide? Let's fly into the night of hell.
> But no. There my father holds the fatal urn
> in his strict hands: they say it is his lot.
> There Minos judges each pale human traveler.
> Ah, how my shade will tremble when he sees
> his daughter led before his eyes, constrained

to avow such grave and various trespasses,
and crimes perhaps unknown in hell.[18]

The second section for discussion will be Phèdre's last lines in the play. In the play's concluding scene, Phèdre speaks with her husband, Theseus. In this dialogue, Phèdre finally acquits Hippolytus of Oenone's false charges and accuses herself. At the last, in a breath which will come no more, Phèdre cries:

Now only through a mist I see the sky
and the husband whom my presence wrongs; and death,
stealing the brightness from my eyes, gives back
to the light, which they defiled, all its purity.
(Act 5, 1641–44)

As with critics of the plays analyzed hitherto, commentators on *Phèdre* likewise may be divided into those who affirm and those who deny the place of moral law. Louis-Léonard Nanéix and Roland Barthes, for example, deemphasize, while Éléonore Zimmerman, on the other hand, emphasizes, the role of moral law in *Phèdre*. The former contend, concomitantly, that divinity constitutes an irrational force in the play, the latter a suprarational one. Simone Weil offers evidence that the latter manner of interpretation is consistent with a Christian esoteric reading of Racine's play.

Nanéix argues only a minor place for moral law in *Phèdre*. Further, he believes the moral law the play does describe is a human construction, not divinely ordained. Generally, Nanéix asserts that Phèdre lives in a world where gods merely play with men.[19] He argues an entire lack of justice in the play on these grounds. He takes the world of the play as a simple polytheistic universe where divine wills continually conflict, catching up and destroying human happiness in the process of these conflicts. Nanéix offers as primary examples of divine maleficence the destructive power of Venus and Neptune. The former divinity instigates Phèdre's unwanted passion for Hippolytus. The latter god causes Hippolytus' death by way of Theseus' ignorant anger against his son, a wrath based on Oenone's deception. There can be no justice in such a world, Nanéix maintains, because in this universe no single divine will publishes a law (211–12).

Yet Nanéix suggests that a moral consciousness characterizes Racine's characters. Nanéix asserts that all the characters believe good exists and that good and evil differ from each other. But this moral consciousness, Nanéix concludes, is purely human, coming as it were from another kind of divinity than Venus and Neptune, a divinity within man and not outside him. "Racine, in short, by means of his characters, summonses divinity to become worthy of the esteem and the veneration of men" (232). Thus Nanéix finds in *Phèdre* a protest against what *is* in the form of a desire for what ought to be. This protest constitutes, for Nanéix, "the only consoling ray, amidst everything which is sadly disquieting in this work" (247–48).

Thus, Nanéix believes that whatever moral sense the play offers resides only in the inner indignation and bewilderment of man himself. Human beings wish, but fail, to find the heavens more just than the earth, the gods nobler than human beings. Nanéix questions, thus, the integrity of Phèdre's self-accusations. He casts aspersions on the cry of self-contempt which informs the "Where hide?" speech. Nanéix interprets as a sign of masochism Phèdre's judgment of herself before the eye of the sun and the underworld: "Phèdre, for the moment, believes in the value of judgments, as if they were based on clear criteria and conformed to the articles of a solidly established code. But we who know as well as Oenone all the immorality which the mythological pantheon cultivates, we wonder if it is not chiefly her masochistic imagination which exposes and dedicates Phaedra to such a formidable Judgment" (141).

Concomitantly, for Nanéix, Phèdre experiences an increasing self-absorption as the play proceeds: "At first a helpless simpleton, she foundered into a kind of lunacy which rendered her very malevolent" (150). Nanéix asserts, then, that there is nothing admirable about Phèdre, including her final lines: "Rejected Phèdre kills others, swallows poison, pronounces a bad confession, and dies egotistically absorbed by concern for the effect of her death on the purity of the day" (210).

According to Nanéix, then, allusions to a moral ideal exist in *Phèdre* in the form of human aspiration. This ideal is shaped and supplied by no religious inspiration, pagan or Christian, but rather by art. "The morality of the work of art, is not to betray Art. Art purifies everything that it touches. The authentic artist makes morality out of immorality, as he makes beauty out of ugliness" (226). Thus, for Nanéix, the moral inspiration at the root of *Phèdre* may be properly called neither Christian nor pagan but, rather, artistic.

Roland Barthes takes Nanéix's aesthetic approach to *Phèdre* one step further by asserting that the content of the play carries no moral implications, artistic or religious. According to Barthes's interpretation, the categories of good and evil do not in any meaningful sense apply to this play.

Barthes asserts Phèdre experiences no objective guilt; Barthes identifies culpability with "interiority" or secrecy.[20] In this play, Barthes maintains, things are not hidden because they are culpable, they are culpable because they are hidden. Language, therefore (the tools of art), rather than moral law, is the arbiter of "good and evil" in the play. According to Barthes, Phèdre's objective guilt—her adultery and her incest—is actually an artificial construction "intended to naturalize the suffering of the secret" (124).

Rather than commenting on Phèdre's references to brightness and light, the actual focus of Phèdre's final lines, Barthes interprets the purport of Phèdre's last words as her restoring movement to the world by means of a motionless death. This death was belatedly but finally released through words. Before the tragedy begins, Phèdre already wants to die, but her death is suspended: Only speech will release this motionless death, restore to the world its "movement" (117). (During the course of the play, Phèdre avows the secret of her passion first to Oenone, then to Hippolytus, and finally to Theseus at play's end.)

For Barthes, man's relationship with the divine in *Phèdre* is a relationship which does not subsist on a moral plane, nor, therefore, is it a relationship where moral law has a place. Always the Racinian language between man and God, for Barthes, is the language of combat or irony or blasphemy; for the very being of God is wickedness (40–41). "Phaedra's entire effort consists in *fulfilling* her transgression, that is, in absolving God" (124). Thus, necessarily, for Barthes, the "Where hide?" speech, in which Phèdre reveals the culmination of a feeling of guilt, reveals ignorance rather than moral sensitivity or, certainly, heroism.

The Racinian heroine's story is a drama of repression, where the character, rather than rebelling against the Father god who keeps her repressed, lives a life of bad faith, by associating him with an Absolute Good. Thus, she never experiences a new birth, a birth of an autonomous human being (52). By taking guilt on herself and thereby retaining her idea of God as good, Phèdre absolves God from what he is in fact responsible for (and not she). Thus Phèdre tragically suffers from a regression unto death. For Barthes, "The hero's guilt is a functional necessity: if man is pure then God is impure and the world falls apart. Hence man must cling to his transgression as his most precious belonging" (46).

The tragic heroine's inferno is not guilt but constriction (20). Her activity is conflict, a conflict actually amoral in kind (Barthes insists on the amoral nature of Phèdre's suffering [30]). Her problem is on the level of structure, not character (30). Finally, as for Nanéix in a lesser sense, in a larger way, for Barthes, art or the human imagination reconciles man with the world. In Racine all the disappointments of the world are taken up and redeemed in speech (50). "Tragedy tends ultimately toward a dialectical function: out of the spectacle of failure it believes it can create a transcendence of failure, and out of the passion of the immediate, a mediation. When all things are destroyed tragedy remains a *spectacle*, that is, a reconciliation with the world" (59–60).

Éléonore Zimmerman offers a far different manner of interpreting Phèdre's guilt feelings, and her dying wish to restore to the day its purity, than Nanéix and Barthes propose. In contradiction of these two critics, Éléonore Zimmerman asserts that moral law, an objective phenomenon, plays a central role in Racine's drama. The gods themselves uphold and undergird moral law. Thus the gods constitute a supra-rational, rather than an irrational, force. These premises necessarily distinguish Zimmerman's critique of *Phèdre* from those of the two modernist critics. In the hands of Nanéix and Barthes, Racine's art and Phèdre's fate become amoral phenomena.

Éléonore Zimmerman carefully categorizes all references to the divine in *Phèdre.* She argues a distinction between the characters' invocations of general gods ("o dieux! justes dieux!") and their invocations of personal gods. The general gods, called upon by major and minor characters alike, are guarantors of social and moral order, guardians of moral law.[21] They protect laws against suicide and incest, laws which guard conjugal fidelity, duty toward children (90). These gods are neither fled from nor defied (92). "They represent fixed guiding marks accepted by all, supernumeraries as principle characters" (92).

Further, according to Zimmerman, an individual god, such as Venus, unlike the general gods, has no reality outside the experience of an individual character; thus, rather than acting as an actual divine force in the play, Venus, for example, represents Phèdre's illicit passion. By the time of Phèdre's final words, it is clear that other personal gods, Minos and the Sun, divinities who closely resemble the general gods themselves, have replaced Venus in Phèdre's soul (106). This fact constitutes a moral triumph. This triumph is made possible as the result of Phèdre's descent into a hell of guilt and self-contempt. This period of intense affliction itself occurs, according to Zimmerman, during the "Where hide?" speech and continues to reveal itself in Phèdre's subsequent revolution against Oenone. (Phèdre believes she has been too easy prey to the immoral counsel of her nurse [106].)

As Venus represents Phèdre's private passion, continuing to follow Zimmerman, Neptune represents Theseus' private anger. There is a time in the play when this god ceases to be part of the mental life of Theseus who had called for the help of Neptune in punishing Hippolytus (94). Thus Zimmerman counters those critics who, on the basis of the behavior of Venus and Neptune, describe the central divine force in Racine's play as being irrational rather than suprarational, existing below, rather than above, the level of reason and morality.

Zimmerman maintains that Racine's play was written within the framework of the general seventeenth-century belief that the greatest liberty lies in desiring the will of God, in accepting the order of things (48–49). Phèdre, for example, affirms the moral order of the world by condemning herself even for an act of wrongdoing which is compulsory. In this self-accusatory attitude she resembles Oedipus. Phèdre believes that her incestuous passion, "no more belonged than Oedipus' parricide and incest" (112). Theseus and Hippolytus, no more than Phèdre, accuse the gods for their own fates (108, 116).

For Zimmerman, Racine's universe is regulated by a divinity which is essentially, if enigmatically, good. The sun symbolizes divine goodness in the play: "The social order...is presented as a universal order in harmony with the cosmic order, as the role which the sun plays suggests, an order approved by the gods and not fashioned arbitrarily by men" (112).

In contradiction of Nanéix and Barthes, who denigrate Phèdre as a character, Zimmerman thus regards Racine's protagonist as an heroic figure who successfully fights a battle between conflicting personal gods. Through deep and great struggle, a battle moral, not amoral, in kind, Phèdre ultimately wins against illicit passion, homicidal anger. She emerges victorious on the side of a Good which is absolute. This Good is symbolized by the sun, which shines as an ideal power throughout Racine's universe. Thus, there is nothing either self-centered (Nanéix) or morally neutral (Barthes) about Phèdre's final words. The love of the light, which Phèdre vocalizes at this point, suggests that her love of the good triumphs at the last:

> Now only through a mist I see the sky
> and the husband whom my presence wrongs;

and death, stealing the brightness from my eyes,
gives back to the light, which they defiled, its purity.
(Act 5, 1641–45)

Yet, despite her belief that a moral law guarded by divinity defines the parameters of Phèdre's story, Zimmerman objects to viewing *Phèdre* as a Christian play. She does so on three grounds: (1) The characters simply accept their lot; they do not ask of God, "Why me?", a question Zimmerman suggests is the natural reaction of one who believes in a loving God; (2) the link with Sophocles marks the play as pre-Christian rather than Christian in spirit; and (3) Phèdre lacks charity toward Oenone; also, Phèdre commits suicide—thus escaping the decrees of God (108, fn. 3).

Although Simone Weil's sapiential metaphysics helps to answer all three of these objections,[22] it is Zimmerman's third point that is of real interest here. By focusing on the fulfillment of God's *decrees* in her discussion of the play's putative Christian nature, Zimmerman indicates a (popular) assumption that any character cast in a Christian mold must keep strictly to a code of moral law. At this point Weil's mystical Christian outlook is particularly helpful.

When Christianity is regarded from the perspective of its central mystery—the cross of Christ—then this religion, like tragedy itself, may be said to take into account the harsh circumstances, including the existence of "psychic matter,"[23] which can prevent a human being from fulfilling divine law even despite his or her own desire to be true to it. The cross, as paradigm of guiltless guilt, offers a model of an obedience to God understood in a mystical rather than a legalistic sense. The attitude of obedience which shines forth on the cross directs itself not toward a code of law but rather toward God himself. This is not a rational but a suprarational obedience, an obedience which pierces through moral law to its divine source.

For most of the play, Phèdre expresses simple horror at her fate as victim of a forbidden passion and its concomitant maleficent desires. Only at the play's close does her egocentric self-disgust, a preoccupation moral in kind, turn to a selfless love of the good, a phenomenon no longer simply moral but supramoral.

Concerning Phèdre's usual, self-absorbed state of soul, Weil says, "There is a certain instinct of self-preservation which encourages us to remain as we are, which rejects progress. It makes us flee the light, because the light effects changes. It does not prevent remorse because there is no light in remorse. On the contrary, remorse is the very movement made to hide oneself.

"In *Phèdre* the moment of remorse is 'Where to hide yourself?'...The moment of repentance: 'all [its] purity'" (*NB*, 269–70).

As we have seen, the "Where hide?" speech, the primary section to which Weil alludes in this passage, occurs directly after Phèdre discovers the existence of a rival to her forbidden love for Hippolytus, the princess Aricie. The speech that articulates Phèdre's painful discovery shows neither complete despair of her own existence;[24] nor a new relaxation of her passion, born of shock at the news of a competitor;[25] nor, as Nanéix proposes, a tendency to masochism. This speech shows simply, as Weil implies, the consummation of her sense of guilt or remorse, a self-contempt manifested already in her very first words in the play (act 1, 158–61; 169–72). By the time of the "Where hide?" speech, Phèdre's remorse, the substance of her affliction, has become intensified to a scarcely bearable degree.

As we have seen, at the news of Hippolytus' love for Aricie, Phèdre sees in her mind's eye a woman who loves Hippolytus innocently. This vision, combined with horror at the desire Phèdre feels within herself to have Aricie destroyed, redoubles her own suffering, her sense of herself as a reject of nature unfit for the light of day. In a frenzy of self-contempt Phèdre seeks concealment in every part of the universe. But where can she hide ("Où me cacher?")? Her ancestor the sun, symbol of purity, reigns over the heavens; the earth itself bears reminders of her sister and mother, fellow prey of Venus; and fate has placed her father Minos as judge of the underworld (act 4, 1277–84). Phèdre's state of humiliation, her feeling of despair and remorse, is complete.

Yet out of this consummate affliction comes a full spiritual victory, one to which her final words bear witness.

"The only way into truth," says Weil, "is through one's own annihilation; through dwelling a long time in a state of extreme and total humiliation" (*SWR*, 331). The blind play of circumstance may at any time turn all one regards and treasures as one's own, all one views as constituting one's very self, into something of the filthiest and most contemptible sort. An experiential understanding of this fact can serve to awaken the soul to the instability of all things human, including even one's own character. Then with revulsion, the soul may be induced to turn itself away from the human, the contingent, the personal, toward the impersonal, the transcendent, the divine.

The power of Venus symbolizes the blind play of necessity in Racine's play. It is through Phèdre's time as Venus' captive, a time of consummate affliction, that Phèdre becomes purified of all self-regard. During the period of her affliction, Phèdre never ceases to love the very good against which her captor militates. Her torments of conscience bear witness to Phèdre's unwavering orientation toward the good. That direction, however, does not aim directly at its object until the final moments before Phèdre dies. Until that time, the afflicted queen's love of the good is mingled with a self-regard which takes the form of remorse. For remorse to transform itself into genuine repentance, a person must transcend a moral level of existence and dwell on a supramoral plane.

A comparison between Weil's attitude toward Phèdre and her opinion of another outcast, the prostitute described in the gospels, illustrates the distinctive nature of repentance, as opposed to remorse.

Of the despised, the degraded prostitute, anointing and shedding tears over the feet of Jesus, Weil says: "Nothing could be purer than her action, which involved complete self-forgetfulness. She had even forgotten that her contact was a pollution.

"To turn toward the good in this way, without any regard for oneself, one must feel in one's very bones the wretchedness of the human condition and the degradation to which the flesh is subjected or exposed.

"The soul must have been pierced through by the bitterness of human misery, to the point where life holds no more hope at all.

"Then the tears which spring from the depths of shame are a pure tribute to the good" (*FLN*, 314–15).

In the concluding scene of Racine's play, similarly, Weil finds in Phèdre an attitude of perfect repentance which one might compare to the self-forgetful shame which Weil believes marks the harlot's approach to Christ. Up until the very final moments of the tragedy, however, as Weil herself suggests, Phèdre's state of soul is not self-forgetful, the mark of genuine repentance, but rather self-preoccupied, weighed down by her own suffering, a suffering moral in kind.

The "Where hide?" speech concludes with Phèdre's explosive accusation against her maid for having helped smooth for Phèdre the path to wrongdoing. The concluding scene of the play follows shortly upon Phèdre's last, most bitter expression of self-contempt, projected onto Oenone. In the final scene, the dying queen rises above a loathing for the evil within her, a contempt which is self-preoccupied, obsessed, therefore, with the desire to hide. There resonates now an open, a courageous, a frank and selfless, a heartbreaking love of the good outside her and beyond her reach. In these words, we may find a perfect self-forgetfulness comparable to that of the prostitute at the feet of Christ. Now Phèdre reveals to Theseus for the first time, the truth of her own behavior from beginning to end, even as she feels the poison she has taken begin to chill her heart.[26]

Thus, as Éléonore Zimmerman suggests, Phèdre's last words imply the ultimate victory of her love of the good, symbolized by her selfless love of the light, associated with Phèdre's ancestor, the sun. Again, in contradiction of the value-neutral or denigrating interpretations of Barthes and Nanéix, respectively, these words are not only morally but even supramorally charged. At the moment of death, Phèdre triumphs over all the instincts within her which had militated against the good. A conflict between a longing to violate divine law, on the one hand, and a desire to revere it, on the other—a battle moral in kind—constitutes Phèdre's affliction. Phèdre's spiritual victory over this affliction may be said to be compatible with the outlook of Christian faith. Although compulsory wrongdoing may lead to a pathetic state of despair, it will not do so, as it does not in the case of Phèdre, if the protagonist's moral wretchedness is purged by an indifference to her own defilement. As her final lines attest, with the heavy weight of degradation upon her, Phèdre is yet able to rejoice sincerely that pure good exists.

Like Oedipus's words of assent to Creon, Phèdre's final lines also offer evidence that, even through a state of moral corrosion, even through a supremely humiliating condition caused by a wrongdoing which is compulsory in kind, a love for the good may triumph. The crucified Christ is also borne down by the weight of a supreme degradation which only moral pollution can bring. Although convinced that he is abandoned to a state of sin on the cross, yet the Christ continues to love the good even from out of the belly of evil. The likeness Oedipus and Phèdre bear to the suffering Christ constitutes evidence that both Sophocles' and Racine's dramas may be regarded as sacred works of art from a Christian perspective.

A heart-breaking transcendence over a conviction of one's own ignominy, a victory over a sin which is felt in all its infamy, though uninvited, can not be discerned either by a morally neutral eye, such as that of the modernist, or by an eye attached to reason alone, such as that of the religious rationalist. It may be discerned only by a person in whom a third, an inner, eye has been actualized. For the flash of this beam, directed toward classical tragic art, we are indebted to the mystical Christian vision of Simone Weil.

By the light of the esoteric dimension of Christianity, tragedies of crime, no less than tragedies of calamity, may be offered as high tragedies with a Christian tone. As tragic justifications of God's ways to man, both kinds of plays evoke not optimism (a rationalistic term) but, rather, religious mystery.

By the glow of Christ's cross, it may be intuited that the justice of the world is constituted, not by a fair distribution of reward and punishment, but rather by the mark of a divine sacrifice willed from the foundation of the world.

Notes

1. See, e.g., Nussbaum's discussion of Euripides' *Hecuba*. According to Nussbaum, only the absence of (reliable) divinity makes possible the tragic fragility of Hecuba's moral character. ("The Betrayal of Convention: A Reading of Euripides' *Hecuba*" in *Fragility of Goodness*, esp. pp. 397–421.)

2. Martin Luther, "A Commentary on St. Paul's Epistle to the Galatians," in *Martin Luther: Selections from His Writings* (1961), p. 136.

3. Anyone who believes that human beings have control over their good and evil actions cannot, except at the risk of self-contradiction, maintain that guiltless guilt (compulsory wrongdoing) is possible. Thus, any critic who opposes the possibility of a Christian tragedy on the grounds that the justice of the Christian God expresses itself by a rational distribution of reward and punishment *ipso facto* bars guiltless guilt from Christian vision. (For a list of rationalist opponents to Christian tragedy, see ch. 2, n. 15.)

4. Sophocles, *Oedipus the King* (1964), lines 835–43. Further references to *Oedipus the King* are to this edition and will be cited in the text.

5. Rather than regarding man and the gods as separate entities, capable of relationship, Cedric Whitman, e.g., suggests that the only viable godhead operative in Sophocles' Oedipus story is Oedipus himself. Otherwise the gods can only be regarded as a form of irrational evil. (*Sophocles: a Study of Heroic Humanism* (1971), esp. pp. 214–16, 129–42). Jean-Pierre Vernant also dismisses the possibility of relationship between man and the gods in the Oedipus story, but without collapsing the two. Rather than serving as the

foundation for moral law, the Sophoclean gods, all-powerful, are above the law. This fact precludes the possibility of serious relationship between the human and the divine, i.e., relationship on moral grounds. ("Ambiguity and Reversal. On the Enigmatic Structure of *Oedipus Rex*," in *Tragedy and Myth in Ancient Greece* (1981), esp. pp. 99–100).

6. Knox, *Oedipus at Thebes*, pp. 49–50. Page numbers of further references to *Oedipus at Thebes* will be found in parentheses after each citation.

7. Bowra, *Sophoclean Tragedy*, p. 205. Page numbers of further references to *Sophoclean Tragedy* will be found in parentheses after each citation.

8. On this point see, e.g., R. C. Jebb, *Sophocles: The Plays and Fragments* (1902), p. xxviii.

9. For examples, see Ehrenberg, *Sophocles and Pericles*; R. P. Winnington-Ingram, ch. 7, "Fate in Sophocles," in *Sophocles: An Interpretation* (1980), esp. pp. 203ff.

10. See Kitto, *Sophocles*, esp. pp. 42ff.

11. Jaffier, protagonist of Weil's *Venise Sauvée*, jeopardizes his own security in a self-sacrificial act of love for the enemy. Simone Weil hoped to make it felt that Jaffier's sacrifice was motivated by a love supernatural in kind (*PVS*, 47). Concomitantly, Weil hoped her play would revive for the first time since ancient Greece the perfection of the Sophoclean hero (*PVS*, 52).

12. Hauerwas, *Community of Character*; Hauerwas, *Truthfulness and Tragedy*; Nussbaum, *Fragility of Goodness*.

13. Kitto, *Sophocles*, pp. 62–63.

14. On this point, see Geoffrey Brereton, *Jean Racine: A Critical Biography* (1951), p. 219; P. Sellier, "Le jansénisme des tragédies de Racine: Réalité où illusion?" *Cahiers de l'Association Internationale des Études Françaises* 31 (1979), p. 135.

15. Jean Racine, Préface to *Phèdre*, in *Théâtre complet* (1960), p. 542, incl. n. 202.

16. Brereton, *Jean Racine*, p. 224.

17. John A. Stone, *Sophocles and Racine* (1964), p. 14.

18. Jean Racine, *Phaedra*, in *Three Plays of Racine* (1961), act 4, lines 1227–31 & 1236–42; 1264–65 & 1268–84. Further citations from *Phaedra* will be from this edition and will be documented in the text.

19. Louis-Léonard Nanéix, *Phèdre l'incomprise: Essai de critique directe* (1977), pp. 210–11. Page numbers of further references to *Phèdre l'incomprise* will be found in parentheses after each citation. The translations from the French are my own.

20. Roland Barthes, *On Racine* (1964), p. 124. Page numbers of further references to *On Racine* will be found in parentheses after each citation.

21. Éléonore Zimmerman, *La Liberté et le destin dans le théâtre de Jean Racine* (1982), pp. 89, 100. Page numbers of further references to *La Liberté* will be found in parentheses after each citation. The translations from the French are my own.

22. (1) For Simone Weil, in all truly great art (in this category she ranks Racine's *Phèdre*, [*IC*, 54]), Christ's own cry, "Why hast thou forsaken me?" will resound through every word. It is in the details of Phèdre's affliction that we may find, according to a Weilian reading, the cry Zimmerman fails to hear because she seeks only a verbal formulation of it. The miseries of a woman torn between an insuperable wish to contravene moral law, on the one hand, and a deep and abiding reverence for that law, on the other, constitute the affliction in this play out of which resonates the silent cry, "Why am I being hurt?" In a Weilian sense, then, "Why have you abandoned me?", though not vocalized in so many words, pierces yet through Phèdre's every line.

(2) In all French theater, Weil maintains, *Phèdre* alone approximates the tragic vision of Sophocles—the alienation and abandonment, the sudden loss of everything that attaches oneself to the world and God: "Woe is unlimited....Tragedy captures this unlimitedness as in a net; it is necessary that it should remain unlimited and yet cease to be so. Relationships of force have got to appear in lightning fashion in the midst of which man loses himself, God, the universe, everything—*Phèdre* is like this, and nothing else in the French theater" (*NB*, 27).

(3a) As regards the matter of Phèdre's suicide, Weil suggests, "Suicide is only licit when it is but apparent, when there is constraint and one is fully conscious of such constraint....We are not defiled by actions from which we are absent in this fashion" (*NB*, 57).

That Phèdre was constrained to suicide may be seriously argued. Even Oenone, Phèdre's constant life support, sees suicide as the only possible action open to Phèdre once she hears of her mistress' incestuous passion (act 1, 337–39). Only news of Theseus' supposed death encourages Oenone to urge Phèdre to think of continuing to live (act 1, 340ff.). Phèdre's despairing condition just before she takes poison also suggests constraint. Panope speaks to Theseus of "[Phèdre's] present wildness. / She has a mortal, desperate look; the white shadow of death is even now in her face....She goes at random with uncertain steps; / her staring eyes no longer know us" (act 5, 1462–64; 1475–76). This detail points to a woman so intensely distraught, even mad, that she seems already to be death's own.

(3b) Further, Phèdre's treatment of Oenone was not necessarily cruel. It would seem, first, that Oenone herself believes she merited Phèdre's angry accusation. Shortly after the "Where shall I hide?" speech, Phèdre accuses her maid of having smoothed for her an unlawful road. This road ultimately led to what Phèdre correctly assumes, at this point, will be the death of Hippolytus. In response to her mistress' angry rebuke, Oenone says, "Ah, Gods, / to serve her I have done all, forsaken all, / And this is my reward? I have well deserved it" (act 4, 1327–29). Secondly, Oenone's subsequent suicide rather increases Phèdre's trouble than calms it. Panope reports to Theseus, "[Oenone's] death has not calmed the Queen: / the trouble seems to grow in her restless soul" (act 4, 1469–70). Thirdly, when Phèdre speaks to Theseus of Oenone's suicide, she does so just before talking of her own suicide. This fact suggests Racine is pointing a contrast (act 5, 1622–40). Phèdre herself, Racine points out, made a choice of a slow and therefore painful death, one which would allow her time to exonerate Hippolytus. Unlike Phèdre, Oenone does not appear to have felt remorse for the libel against Theseus' son (act 4, 1295–1306). Unlike Phèdre, Oenone chose a swift suicide which shows no concern to try to undo any wrong she had done.

23. On "psychic" or "non-tangible" matter, see the Weilian interpretation of *Oedipus the King* in the first section of this chapter, pp. 125–27.

24. Lucien Goldmann, *The Hidden God* (1964), p. 390.

25. Stone, *Sophocles and Racine*, p. 68.

26. On the problem of Phèdre's suicide, see n. 22 (3a), above.

Conclusion
Toward a Transcultural Poetics

Simone Weil's tragic religion, as her tragic conception of art, suggests an essential harmony between tragic vision and the esoteric dimension of Christianity. Specifically, from Weil's perspective, tragic art may be said to illuminate the central mystery of the Christian faith, the cross of Christ. The cross may be offered as a supreme model of affliction, a suffering consummate in kind. This torment the crucified Christ transcended when he sustained a perfect love for the Father at the moment when he believed the Father had abandoned him to the sins of the world. When the human being maintains a love for the good in affliction, even at the time of his own dereliction, he gains experiential knowledge of Christ's cross. From a Christian perspective, the human being thereby gains knowledge of God. This contact with God opens up the very secret of the universe. In the realm of poetry, only certain works of tragic drama evoke the central Christian mystery. Tragic poetry alone enshrines the cruciform beauty of the world.

The four classical tragedies this study examines offer the possibility of piercing through moral law to a sacred or supernatural source. This grace comes violently. This unveiling, only affliction, unutterable torment, effects. The conception of tragic suffering as a yielder of rational insight (Aristotle), or as a route to aesthetic redemption (Nietzsche), in certain respects, shortchanges or even falsifies tragic masterpieces.

In a Platonic light, tragedy regards suffering as a means neither to rational insight nor to aesthetic redemption but rather as a path to obtaining a boon which is suprarational rather than rational (Aristotle) or irrational (Nietzsche). The suprarational benefit which tragedy yields is knowledge of a supernatural good. This knowledge may be called authentically rather than spuriously religious. Rather than ignoring the moral dimension of life, as romantic "inspiration" does, tragic wisdom both affirms and also transcends the categories of good and evil. From this perspective, the tragedies examined in this study may be called genuinely sacred works of art. Concomitantly, these plays reveal an important point of contact between the tragic outlook and the Christian vision in its esoteric dimension. Sacred art attempts to justify a world that contains suffering and evil not by an appeal to reason but through an evocation of the suprarational, an invitation to contemplate religious mystery.

Weil's call to meditate upon tragic drama from the perspective of Christ's cross is the cry of the true Christian mystic. Rather than focusing on the joyous benefits the cross of Christ brings—release from sin and its effects—the Christian mystic would love God for himself alone, without regard to personal benefit. Weil's mystical thoughts on tragedy help to articulate her belief that one cannot love the crucified God purely without having knowledge of his sufferings. In this sense, it may be said, tragic art contains deep within it the pearl of the knowledge of God.

Ananda Coomaraswamy, the traditionalist art critic *par excellence*, has suggested that God is the subject of all truly great art.[1] As we have seen, in our Weilian approach to tragic drama, faith in God entails belief in the existence and the union of a Goodness and a Truth which are absolute. Unlike the traditionalist view of literature, the theories of literature which reign today deny the existence of any truth or goodness which is not culturally dependent and therefore relative. This skepticism concerning the existence of an absolute good results in a value-neutral outlook. In our conversations concerning tragedy, we have seen consistently the modernist's propensity to sidestep the categories of good and evil in his discussion of a literary work.

The two most recent schools of literary criticism, structuralism and poststructuralism, exemplify in an extreme form the modern tendency to evade life's moral dimension. Contrary to the traditional point of view, the structuralist and the poststructuralist critic attempt to legitimate pure speculation, thought detached from human experience. In contradiction of these literary theorists, a number of important twentieth-century thinkers have asserted that purely abstract ideas harbor destructive power. Concepts cut off from human life are dangerous because they are necessarily value-neutral.

Indeed, Elie Wiesel, the contemporary Jewish sage, a survivor of the holocaust, holds modern thinkers responsible, in part, for the destructiveness of the Nazi regime. In a recent address on tolerance and learning, Wiesel suggested that whenever thought becomes theoretical, detached from life, it divorces itself form ethical concerns and thus leaves a dangerous void where moral conscience should be.[2] Simone Weil posits, similarly, that the amoral, and consequently irrelevant, vision of modern literature was a contributing factor to the disasters of World War II: "Writers do not have to be professors of morals, but they do have to express the human condition and nothing concerns human life so essentially, for every man at every moment, as good and evil. When literature becomes deliberately indifferent to the opposition of good and evil it betrays its function and forfeits all claim to excellence" (*SNL*, 168–69). T. S. Eliot, another twentieth-century traditionalist, associates the theological dearth of this century with its ethical unease. He thus warns against a literature pervaded by the antisupernaturalism, the secularism of the age.[3]

The negative consequences of intellectual sophistry call out for remedy. I believe a traditionalist poetics might serve the healing function in literary circles today which Socratic and Platonic thought provided in fifth-century B.C. Athens. I would like briefly to defend this assertion. I hope, in this way, to draw out the significance of this Platonic and mystical

Christian approach to tragic literature. Concomitantly, the unashamed supernaturalism of this book will endeavor to explain itself.

I will first suggest parallels between ancient Greek sophistry, on the one hand, and contemporary literary theory, on the other. By way of Plato, I will then look to the religious traditions to supply the foundation for a poetics which counters the value-neutral orientation of contemporary literary criticism.

Like the debate between the sophists and Socrates/Plato itself, the following discussion will concern truth and goodness. It will become evident that without grounds for believing that these two mutually dependent values are absolute, the very foundation and significance of literature falls: the act of communication between author and reader. The benign purposiveness of an act of writing alone ensures the autonomy of writer and reader alike. Without universally meaningful content, no work of literature, or literary theory, can be more than the product of private wish fulfillment, fancy, or illusion. The very idea of communication between author and reader becomes irrelevant in such a case.

Further, when sophistry reigns in the world of letters, an author is likely to become enslaved to, rather than to wield for his own purpose, the language which his society both creates and controls. A reader, like an author, will necessarily become depersonalized, then, as well. The enslavement of author and reader is a natural consequence of relativist philosophy, because all forms of relativism, from the most mild to the most extreme, inherently jeopardize the autonomy of the individual. A single human being, without the defense of an appeal to truth or goodness, cannot defend himself against the will of a group.

Here, then, is the story of how philosophical sophistry has invaded the domain of literary theory to the point where it has undermined the relationship between author and reader. What sophistry destroys, however, the intuition of an absolute good may restore. By story's end, a supernaturalist literary theory will appear robed in light.

The gentle skepticism of Protagoras resembles, to a degree, the outlook of the contemporary structuralist critic.

Protagoras, the first influential Greek sophist, proposed that man is the measure of all things. Whatever exists exists as a result of human, not divine, impetus. Thus, all "truth" is derived from a particular human society, a particular culture. Truth, then, actually consists of fictions, group fictions, which enable societies to keep order and therefore to endure. Protagoras, however, does not yet attack language as a valid source of communication within a given society, as Gorgias, a fellow sophist, will do; nor does he substitute for the idea of goodness the power relations in a particular culture, like Thrasymachus. Indeed, Protagoras respects social structures. He regards each of them as a locus of order, even if, as a sophist or culturalist, he believes this order is created by the practical adherence to convention rather than by reverence for any actual, unchangeable moral values. The universality of moral norms Protagoras' knowledge of the diversity of cultural mores caused him to disbelieve in. The sophists, generally, shared this view.[4]

Modern structuralist criticism operates according to premises which resemble those of Protagoras in certain ways. Structuralists respect the "meanings" of a given society, as conveyed through socially created signs and symbols, and they interpret literary texts according to them. These meanings are regarded as relative and therefore lacking in "truth" in any universal sense; yet the system of language according to which a society operates is, respectfully, accepted as a basis for interpreting literary texts. Verbal signs are regarded as arbitrary, entirely a matter of social convention, therefore having a purely relative, rather than universal, import. Yet the structuralist views these signs as systematic. In a practical sense, language and other sign systems provide any given culture with a source of coherence which is useful.[5]

Gorgias deepens the relativism of Protagoras, a relativism which contemporary structuralism in some ways evokes. For Gorgias, "truth" is not relative, as for Protagoras; rather, there is no truth. Gorgias suggests that words themselves are symbols or signs which symbolize or signify nothing. Comparably, the contemporary deconstructionist takes one step further the skepticism of the structuralist. The determinate meanings the structuralist affirms are, for the deconstructionist, indeterminate. All language lacks an extratextual purpose which might center it. Thus the decentered play of words obviates even meaning of a strictly cultural kind. "We can never in any instance of speech or writing, have a fixed and decidable present meaning....the differential play (*jeu*) of language does produce the 'effects' of decidable meanings in an utterance or text, but...these effects are illusory" (227).

The skepticism of the sophists takes a third and final turn with Thrasymachus. For Thrasymachus, because there is no truth, there can be no moral values. If there is no universal definition of the human—but only diverse "human" cultures—there can be no ought for behavior. Standards of behavior, a society's laws, a ruling class fabricates in order to sustain its own power. Thus, Thrasymachus concludes, might makes right.

Although the New Historicists, the most influential poststructuralist school today, do not, like Thrasymachus, explicitly propose an amoral superman—indeed, as we will see, there exist among this group examples of sincere concern for the oppressed—yet the tendency of the New Historicism is to assume that ideology, power relations between social classes, is the fundamental reality. What prescientistic literary theorists commonly regarded as literary themes of a universal moral kind, New Historicists describe as political "representations" which "serve mainly to reproduce, confirm, and propagate the power structures of domination and subordination which characterizes a given society" (249). The tacit substitution of strong–weak for good–evil as the means by which a literary text may best be understood is the offspring of a premise close to that of a nihilist like Thrasymachus. Thrasymachus' nihilism lies latent already in the gentler sophistry of Protagoras, as New Historicist poststructuralism is as much a deepening of as a continued revolt against structuralism.

As the conclusions of Thrasymachus indicate, when the human is identified with the collective, the will to power will assert itself. Thus, when it is assumed, as the sophist assumes, that the human being is a cultural product, it is unlikely that the individual will retain his freedom. The most recent forms of literary theory themselves point to the loss of freedom as a consequence of denying the possibility of serious truth claims. According to structuralist and post-structuralist alike, neither author nor reader possesses liberty. This enslavement occurs, I suggest, because purposive communication between them has become impossible.

According to structuralism, for example, the author is dead.[6] "The mind of an author is described as imputed 'space' within which the impersonal, 'always-already' existing system of literary language, conventions, codes, and rules of combination gets precipitated into a particular text" (281). For the structuralist, the reader replaces the author as central agent, but even the reader loses his personality. Rather than the feelings and thoughts of a flesh-and-blood human being, "the impersonal process of reading by bringing into play the requisite conventions, codes, and expectations, makes literary sense of the sequence of words, phrases, and sentences that constitute a text" (281). Thus, in a literary realm where there is neither truth nor goodness, cultural systems dominate the individual.

For the deconstructionist, also, reader and author alike are virtual nonentities. All readings are misreadings, for "one cannot get beyond the sequence of verbal signs or anything standing outside of, and independent of, the language system that constitutes the text...[including] the intention of its speaker or writer to express a determinate signification" (225–56). Both author and reader become the pawns of a signifying system which can not signify anything outside itself.

Finally, the New Historicist contends that authors and readers both are "shaped and positioned by the conditions and ideological formation of their own era. All claims, therefore, for the possibility of a disinterested and objective interpretation and valuation of a literary text...are among illusions of a humanistic idealism" (251). If an author and reader are themselves unwitting products of ideology, any intentional communication between them becomes impossible. Here, again, the collective crushes the individual under its weight.

In ancient Greece, already, Socrates suggests that sophistical skepticism enchains the human being. A relative truth and goodness draws the individual into a swamp of self-will and indecision which weakens his resistance to collective power. In a famous allegory, Socrates' great pupil, Plato, himself suggests a means of escape from the enslavement which he, like Socrates, believed sophistry causes. The route toward freedom, Plato maintains, is painful. For Plato, as for his wise mentor, human liberation consists in a shocking encounter of the whole being with a reality which is both absolute and good. Intuition of an unconditioned reality, the sole means to authentic liberation from cultural domination, only a person marked by heroic courage may attain firsthand. As we have seen in the discussion of Plato's famous allegory of the cave in chapter 1, for Plato, the liberating encounter with an absolute good is not possible without a courageous willingness to face what is real. Only once a hard-won knowledge of external reality has been attained will the individual self be able to rise above the circumambient world—a given culture and the language by which it operates—to find his way outside the cave of relativity to a supernatural reality, one that imparts an unconditioned strength.

From a Platonic perspective, then, it is the contemporary literary theorist's urge to flee an examination of real life which, today, dooms author and reader alike to domination by a cultural force. Both structuralist and poststructuralist, indeed, disconnect the act of literary communication from the real world of human experience. The structuralist, for example, finds the significance of literature not in the human experience it mirrors, but rather in the linguistic system of which it partakes. Concomitantly, for him, literature holds no function distinct from other forms of writing.

Similarly, it is the alogical thread which unwinds all apparent logic, and not its ability to reflect reality, that attracts the deconstructionist to a literary text. Thus, for the deconstructionist, also, there is nothing either privileged or unique about literature. A poetic text constitutes only one of many different kinds of *écriture* (writing).

Finally, it is not its ability to imitate human life and promote reflection upon its problems but literature's representation of the ideology, the power relations, of a given culture that interests the New Historicist. Thereby, this species of critic also views literature as a form of discourse indistinct from other forms—historical, political, philosophical.

From a Platonic perspective, the lack of interest all three types of theorists show for human life goes hand in hand with their value-neutral orientation—their general lack of ethical concern. We discern here yet another instance of the tendency Simone Weil found to be common among writers in this century: the urge to escape into an artificial world where problems of life, including and especially the moral problem, are evaded. For Weil, this escapism evinces a lack of responsibility. As Elie Wiesel suggests, this flight into theory leads to a moral void which everywhere has consequences. For Plato, this tendency, the fruit of intellectual cowardice, prevents discovery of what is really real: a good absolute in kind. Possession of supernatural wisdom constitutes the only reliable means by which the individual may be liberated from oppression by larger, group forces.

As we have seen in our discussions of classical tragedy, there exists today a literary theory whose premises oppose those of modernist thinkers. To this theory we will now look for a means of relieving the gloom of contemporary criticism. This refreshing outlook follows both Plato and the religious traditions in significant ways. The outlook to which we refer is, of course, the traditionalist.

In opposition to the escapist tendency of structuralism and poststructuralism, the whole purpose of art and art theory, for the traditionalist, is to convey truth about human existence, including its deepest, most mysterious dimensions. Only a torturous death-of-the-ego, the fruit of a head-on encounter with the world outside the ego, may lead to an unveiling of that which is really real. The ultimate reality, rationally indescribable though evocable through metaphor, is not cultural and therefore relative but transcendent (transcultural) and therefore absolute. Nor is this ultimate reality, the realm of mystery, value-neutral. The mystic intuits a reality which is good.

Thus, the traditionalist affirms the existence of a mysterious transcendent realm whose reality concerns every human being. This fact enables the enlightened poet to speak, if metaphorically, yet with intention, with purpose. In turn, the poet's audience, on the receiving end, benefits, as an individual, from the communication. The benign purposiveness of the act of literary communication mystical intuition enables. Structuralist and poststructuralist, we have seen, deny the possibility of either intentional purpose or reliable reception in the act of writing and reading. They thus depersonalize author and reader alike. This enslavement of the individual, sophistical skepticism makes inevitable. Only an intuition of a universal truth, a good without condition, could legitimately free persons on both ends of the act of literary communication.

But what specifically is the content, contained in traditional works of literature, which liberates the individual? The esoteric, or mystical, rather than the exoteric, or legalistic, dimension of the world's religious traditions enshrines a twofold, universal wisdom, a knowledge attainable only through an experience of the whole being: (1) There is a reality which exists above and beyond the human, the cultural, which may be intuited: this reality is good; (2) the dignity and liberation of man lies in his ability to make contact with this reality through self-renunciation or love.

According to the religious traditions, only a couragcous overcoming of the ego or the natural self—a painful, moral process—may yield intuition of a transcendent good. The natural dimension of the personality is linked to society or culture; it leads to the drive for power. Spiritual knowledge, a knowledge attained through an experience of the whole being, overcomes the ego, which is the source of anxiety and social oppression. The awakening or enlightening of the supernatural Self to the existence of a Good which exists above and beyond human beings relaxes the ego. This state of relaxation may be identified as a state of kenosis (self-emptying) or humility. Thus, according to the religious traditions, generally, humility before an Absolute reality may be said to constitute the source of goodness in the human world. Humility's opposite, force, constitutes the fountain of evil. Thus, in this sense, good and evil may be regarded as universal.[7] Taken in this way, the possibility of mysterious encounter with a transcendent reality—the life source of the religious traditions—may offer in contemporary times the hope Socratic and Platonic thought furnished in their own. By unveiling the hidden face of truth, a tender countenance, the great religions afford the basis for a universal morality (*GG*, 164). Concomitantly, they provide real hope for the existence of the truth content which any authentic form of communication requires.

A traditional literary perspective may not only restore freedom to author and reader by providing a benign, meaningful content to the literary work which draws them together, but it also reinfuses literature with the qualities proper to it. Literature can communicate supernatural intuition in a way in which other kinds of writing cannot. Unlike the language of history or philosophy or even theology, poetry is the language of symbol. Besides silence, symbol is the only way human beings have to refer, however inadequately, to a transcendent realm.[8] Symbols may, of course, include whole stories as, for example, the parables of Jesus show.

The traditional perspective may restore literature and literary theory not only on a transcultural but on a cultural level as well. There is no need to say that any meaningful communication between author and reader must concern a content of a transcultural kind. Rather, this, the highest form of communication, guarantees the reliability of all other forms, including communication regarding a human community. In the manner, again, of Plato's famous allegory, insight gleaned from the sun of religious intuition casts light into the cave of biosocial reality. For example, whereas the New Historicism may be regarded as inclining toward nihilistic enslavement, at times an individual New Historicist expresses sincere social concern. For example, a Marxist New Historicist may selflessly insist that critics ought not merely objectively to describe a political ideology at work: Rather, they ought to make an appeal for the alleviation of oppression. This literary theorist's plea for the good, for self-emptying on the part of the strong for the weak, is a cultural or social way of communicating the same value which a transcultural literary theory conveys in its essence. The common attitude of religious worship and social concern is humility before what is good. Similarly, whenever a feminist New Historicist makes a pure-hearted appeal for the dissolution of patriarchy, she also makes use of a transcultural principle: She expresses confidence that, against nature, the empowered will empty themselves on behalf of the powerless.

Any genuine cry to alleviate social oppression is a deliberate, coherent cry, one which requires and evinces real and free communication between author and reader. Thus, apparently without realizing it, the socially concerned New Historicist departs from the very premises of the movement to which he or she purports to belong. The communication between socially concerned author and reader occurs because the content of the communication is not value-neutral but good, not dehumanized but human. The benign, purposive communication such critics hope for may be assured because, ultimately, its content is not culturally but, rather, transculturally derived.

Rather than rational, moral descriptions of social or cultural reality, the works of tragic drama discussed in this book evoke the suprarational, the supramoral. These dramas furnish extended metaphors, stories of love for a good which is absolute, sustained in the depths of affliction. These tragic narratives offer hope that unalterable pain may have a use, a meaning. In these works unutterable suffering purifies an individual's capacity to love. Even when robbed of all earthly objects of love, the tragic protagonist's care for the good remains. These dramas, thus, evoke the sense of wonder. The transcendent orientation of these four tragedies, concealed by modernist readings, the light of Simone Weil's mystical Christian Platonism helpfully and hopefully reveals.

Notes

1. Coomaraswamy, *Christian and Oriental Philosophy of Art*, p. 20. See also Livingston, *Traditional Theory of Literature*, pp. 56, 102–3.

2. Elie Wiesel's address on tolerance and learning to the Library of Congress was broadcast 9 July 1991 on C-SPAN.

3. Eliot, "Religion and Literature," pp. 343–54.

4. I base this short sketch of the Greek sophists on Samuel Enoch Stumpf's *Socrates to Sartre: A History of Philosophy* (1975), ch. 2, "Socrates and the Sophists: The Problems of Truth and Goodness."

5. I draw my summaries of structuralism and the two most influential forms of poststructuralism (deconstruction and the New Historicism) from the standard formulations provided in Abrams, *Glossary of Literary Terms*. Page numbers of direct quotations from *Glossary of Literary Terms* will be found in parentheses after each citation.

6. I use here the dramatic phrase of Roland Barthes, taken from "The Death of the Author," quoted in Abrams, *Glossary of Literary Terms*, p. 281.

7. For the traditionalist conception of a universal moral ideal, one identical with knowledge of a transcendent good, see Nasr, *Knowledge and the Sacred*, ch. 5, "Man, Pontifical and Promethean." Note, for example, the following key passage:

"That man who remains man and continues to survive here and there even during this period of eclipse of spirituality and the desacralization of life is the being who remains aware of his destiny which is transcendence and the function of his intelligence which is knowledge of the Absolute....He knows that the grandeur of man does not lie in his cunning cleverness or titanic creations but resides most of all in the incredible power to empty himself of himself, to cease to exist in the initiatic sense, to participate in that state of spiritual poverty and emptiness which permits him to experience Ultimate Reality" (p. 182).

8. On symbolism as the language of tradition, see, e.g., Nasr, *Knowledge and the Sacred*, p. 153; Livingston, *Traditional Theory of Literature*, pp. 57–60.

Works Cited

1. Simone Weil: Primary Sources

Écrits de Londres et dernières lettres. Paris: Gallimard, 1957.

First and Last Notebooks. Trans. Richard Rees. London: Oxford University Press, 1970.

Gateway to God. Ed. David Raper. Glasgow: William Collins, 1974.

Gravity and Grace. Trans. Arthur Wills. [1952.] New York: Octagon Books, 1987.

Intimations of Christianity among the Ancient Greeks. Trans. Elizabeth Geissbuhler. London: Routledge & Kegan Paul, 1957.

The Notebooks of Simone Weil. Trans. Arthur Wills. 2 vols. New York: Putnam, 1956.

On Science, Necessity, and the Love of God. Trans. Richard Rees. Oxford: Oxford University Press, 1968.

Oppression and Liberty. Trans. Arthur Wills and John Petrie. Amherst: University of Massachusetts Press, 1973.

Poèmes suivis de Venise sauvée. Paris: Gallimard, 1968.

Seventy Letters. Trans. Richard Rees. New York: Oxford University Press, 1965.

The Simone Weil Reader. Ed. George A. Panichas. New York: David McKay, 1977.

Two Moral Essays. Ed. Ronald Hathaway. Wallingford, PA: Pendle Hill Pamphlets, 1981.

Waiting for God. Trans. Emma Craufurd. [1951.] New York: Harper, 1973.

2. Simone Weil: Secondary Sources

Blum, Lawrence A., and Victor J. Seidler. *A Truer Liberty: Simone Weil and Marxism.* New York: Routledge, 1990.

Little, J. P. *Simone Weil: A Bibliography.* London: Grant & Cutler, 1973.

———. *Simone Weil: A Supplement.* London: Grant & Cutler, 1979.

Loades, Ann. "Simone Weil and Antigone: Innocence and Affliction." In *Simone Weil's Philosophy of Culture: Readings toward a Divine Humanity*, ed. Richard Bell, 277–94. New York: Cambridge University Press, 1993.

Nevin, Thomas. *Simone Weil: Portrait of a Self-Exiled Jew.* Chapel Hill: University of North Carolina Press, 1991.

Pétrement, Simone. *La Vie de Simone Weil.* 2 vols. Paris: Fayard, 1973.

Springsted, Eric O. *Christus Mediator: Platonic Mediation in the Thought of Simone Weil.* Chico, California: Scholars Press, 1983.

———. *Simone Weil and the Suffering of Love.* Cambridge, MA: Cowley Press, 1986.

Vetö, Miklos. "The Ethics of Simone Weil." Thesis, Oxford University, 1964.

3. Literature and Religion

Brémond, Henri. *Prière et poésie.* Paris: Bernard Grasset, 1926.

Coomaraswamy, Ananda K. *Christian and Oriental Philosophy of Art.* New York: Dover, 1956.

Eliot, T. S. "Religion and Literature." In *Selected Essays,* 92–115. London: Faber & Faber, 1946.

Gunn, Giles. *The Culture of Criticism and the Criticism of Culture.* Oxford: Oxford University Press, 1987.

———. *The Interpretation of Otherness: Literature, Religion, and the American Imagination.* New York: Oxford University Press, 1979.

Hesla, David. "Religion and Literature: The Second Stage." *Journal of the American Academy of Religion* 46(2): 181–92 (1978).

Jasper, David. *The Study of Literature and Religion: An Introduction.* Minneapolis: Fortress Press, 1989.

Killinger, John. *The Fragile Presence: Transcendence in Modern Literature.* Philadelphia: Fortress Press, 1973.

Livingston, Ray. *The Traditional Theory of Literature.* Minneapolis: University of Minnesota Press, 1962.

Lodge, Rupert. *Plato's Theory of Art.* London: Routledge & Kegan Paul, 1953.

Lynch, Father William. *Christ and Apollo: The Dimensions of the Literary Imagination.* New York: Sheed & Ward, 1960.

Maritain, Jacques. *Creative Intuition in Art and Poetry.* New York: Pantheon Books, 1953.

Murdoch, Iris. *The Fire and the Sun: Why Plato Banished the Artists.* Oxford: Clarendon Press, 1977.

Perotti, James L. *Heidegger on the Divine: The Thinker, the Poet, and God.* Athens, OH: Ohio University Press, 1974.

Scott, Nathan A. *The Broken Center: Studies in the Theological Horizon of Modern Literature.* New Haven: Yale University Press, 1966.

———. "The Modern Experiment in Criticism: A Theological Approach." In *The New Orpheus: Essays toward a Christian Poetic*, ed. Nathan Scott, 141–71. New York: Sheed & Ward, 1964.

———. *Negative Capability: Studies in the New Literature and the Religious Situation.* New Haven: Yale University Press, 1969.

———. *The Poetics of Belief.* Chapel Hill: University of North Carolina Press, 1985.

———. *The Wild Prayer of Longing: Poetry and the Sacred.* New Haven: Yale University Press, 1971.

Van der Leeuw, Gerardus. *Sacred and Profane Beauty: The Holy in Art.* New York: Holt, Rinehart & Winston, 1963.

Von Balthasar, Hans Urs. *The Glory of the Lord: A Theological Aesthetics.* Ed. Joseph Fessio & John Riches. 7 vols. San Francisco: Ignatius Press, 1982–c.1989.

Webb, Eugene. *The Dark Dove: The Sacred and the Secular in Modern Literature.* Seattle: University of Washington Press, 1975.

Woodhouse, A. S. P. *The Poet and His Faith: Religion and Poetry in England from Spenser to Eliot and Auden.* Chicago: University of Chicago Press, 1965.

Wright, T. R. *Theology and Literature.* New York: Basil Blackwell, 1988.

4. Tragedy

Aeschylus. *The Oresteian Trilogy.* Trans. Philip Vellacott. Baltimore: Penguin, 1969.

Aristotle. *Poetics.* In *A New Aristotle Reader*, ed. J. L. Ackrill, 540–56. Princeton: Princeton University Press, 1987.

Auden, W. H. "The Christian Tragic Hero: Contrasting Captain Ahab's Doom and Its Classic Greek Prototype." In *Tragedy: Modern Essays in Criticism*, ed. Laurence

Michael and Richard B. Sewall, 234–48. Englewood Cliffs, NJ: Prentice-Hall, 1963.

Barbour, John. *Tragedy as a Critique of Virtue: The Novel and Ethical Reflection.* Chico, California: Scholars Press, 1984.

Barnet, Sylvan. "Some Limitations of a Christian Approach to Shakespeare." In *Tragedy: Modern Essays in Criticism*, ed. Laurence Michel and Richard B. Sewall, 199–209. Englewood Cliffs, NJ: Prentice-Hall, 1963.

Barthes, Roland. *On Racine.* Trans. Richard Howard. New York: Hill and Wang, 1964.

Bate, Walter Jackson, ed. "Classical Antiquity." In *Criticism: The Major Texts*, 13–76. San Francisco: Harcourt Brace Jovanovich, 1970.

Battenhouse, Roy. *Shakespearean Tragedy: Its Art and Its Christian Premises.* Bloomington: Indiana University Press, 1969.

Booth, Stephen. *King Lear, Macbeth, Indefinition, and Tragedy.* New Haven: Yale University Press, 1983.

Bowra, C. M. *Sophoclean Tragedy.* Oxford: Oxford University Press, 1947.

Bradley, A. C. "Hegel's Theory of Tragedy." In *Hegel on Tragedy*, ed. Anne & Henry Paolucci, 367–88. Westport, CT: Greenwood Press, 1962.

Bradley, A. C. *Shakespearean Tragedy: Lectures on Hamlet, Othello, King Lear, Macbeth.* London: Macmillan, 1949.

Brereton, Geoffrey. *Jean Racine: A Critical Biography.* Toronto: Cassell, 1951.

Brooke, Nicholas. "On Moral Structure vs. Experience." In *Twentieth Century Interpretations of King Lear*, ed. Janet Adelman, 126–27. Englewood Cliffs, NJ: Prentice-Hall, 1978. Originally published in Nicholas Brooke, *Shakespeare: King Lear*, 58–60 (London: Edward Arnold, 1963).

Campbell, Lewis. *Tragic Drama in Aeschylus, Sophocles, and Shakespeare.* London: John Murray, 1904.

The Chronicle History of King Leir: The Original of Shakespeare's 'King Lear.' Ed. Sidney Lee. London: Chatto & Windus, 1909.

Cox, Roger. *Between Earth and Heaven: Shakespeare, Dostoevsky, and the Meaning of Christian Tragedy.* San Francisco: Holt, Rinehart and Winston, 1969.

Ehrenberg, Victor. *Sophocles and Pericles.* Oxford: Basil Blackwell, 1954.

Elton, WIlliam R. *"King Lear" and the Gods.* Lexington: University Press of Kentucky, 1988.

Frye, Northrop. *Anatomy of Criticism: Four Essays.* Princeton: Princeton University Press, 1957.

Gill, R. B. "The Forms of Christian Tragedy." *Bucknell Review* 26(2): 74–83 (1982).

Goldmann, Lucien. *The Hidden God.* New York: Humanities Press, 1964.

Greene, William Chase. *Moira: Fate, Good, and Evil in Greek Thought.* Cambridge: Harvard University Press, 1944.

Hauerwas, Stanley. *A Community of Character.* Notre Dame, IN: Univeristy of Notre Dame Press, 1981.

———. *Truthfulness and Tragedy.* Notre Dame, IN: University of Notre Dame Press, 1977.

Hazelton, Roger. "Tragedy and Providence." *Religion in Life* 31 (1962): 254–63.

Hesla, David. "Greek and Christian Tragedy: Notes toward a Theology of Literary History." In *Art/Literature/Religion: Life on the Borders*, ed. Robert Detweiler, 71–87. Chico, California: Scholars Press, 1983.

Hogan, James C. *A Commentary on the Plays of Sophocles.* Carbondale: Southern Illinois University Press, 1991.

Humphreys, W. Lee. *The Tragic Vision and the Hebrew Tradition.* Philadelphia: Fortress Press, 1985.

Hunt, Barbara. *The Paradox of Christian Tragedy.* Troy, NY: Whitston, 1985.

Hunter, Robert. *Shakespeare and the Mystery of God's Judgments.* Athens: University of Georgia Press, 1976.

Jaeger, Werner. *Archaic Greece/The Mind of Athens.* Trans. Gilbert Highet. Vol. 1 of *Paideia: The Ideals of Greek Culture.* New York: Oxford University Press, 1965.

Jaspers, Karl. *Tragedy Is Not Enough.* Boston: Beacon Press, 1952.

Jebb, R. C. *Sophocles: The Plays and Fragments.* Cambridge: Cambridge University Press, 1902.

Kitto, H. D. F. *Sophocles: Dramatist and Philosopher.* London: Oxford University Press, 1958.

Knox, Bernard. *The Heroic Temper: Studies in Sophoclean Tragedy.* Los Angeles: University of California Press, 1964.

———. *Oedipus at Thebes.* New Haven: Yale University Press, 1957.

La B. Cherbonnier, Edmond. "Biblical Faith and the Idea of Tragedy." In *The Tragic Vision and the Christian Faith,* ed. Nathan A. Scott Jr., 23–56. New York: Association Press, 1957.

Lings, Martin. *The Secret of Shakespeare.* [1966.] Wellinborough, UK: Aquarian Press, 1984.

Lloyd-Jones, Hugh. *The Justice of Zeus.* Los Angeles: University of California Press, 1971.

Nanéix, Louis-Léonard. *Phèdre l'incomprise: Essai de critique directe.* Paris: La Pensée Universelle, 1977.

Niebuhr, Reinhold. *Beyond Tragedy: Essays on the Christian Interpretation of History.* New York: Scribner, 1937.

Nietzsche, Friedrich. "The Birth of Tragedy." In *Basic Writings of Nietzsche*, trans. Walter Kaufmann, 15–144. New York: Modern Library, 1968.

Nussbaum, Martha C. *The Fragility of Goodness: Luck and Ethics in Greek Tragedy and Philosophy*. Cambridge: Cambridge University Press, 1986.

Paolucci, Anne, and Henry Paolucci, eds. *Hegel on Tragedy*. Westport, CT: Greenwood Press, 1962.

Racine, Jean. *Phaedra*. In *Three plays of Racine*, trans. George Dillon, 126–80. Chicago: University of Chicago Press, 1961.

———. Préface to *Phèdre*. In *Théâtre complet*, ed. Maurice Rat, 540–42. Paris: Éditions Garnier Frères, 1960.

Raphael, D. D. *The Paradox of Tragedy*. Bloomington: Indiana University Press, 1959.

Reinhardt, Karl. *Sophocles*. Trans. Hazel Harvey and David Harvey. Oxford: Basil Blackwell, 1979.

Richards, I. A. *Principles of Literary Criticism*. New York: Harcourt Brace, 1925.

Ricoeur, Paul. *The Symbolism of Evil*. Trans. Emerson Buchanan. New York: Harper & Row, 1967.

Roberts, David E. "Christian Faith and Greek Tragedy." *Religion in Life* 1(18): 79–88 (1948).

Roberts, Preston T. "A Christian Theory of Dramatic Tragedy." *Journal of Religion* 31(1): 1–20 (1951).

Sellier, P. "Le jansénisme des tragédies de Racine: Réalité où illusion?" *Cahiers de l'Association Internationale des Études Françaises* 31 (1979): 135–48.

Sewall, Richard. *The Vision of Tragedy*. New Haven: Yale University Press, 1959.

Shakespeare, William. *The Tragedy of King Lear*. In *The Riverside Shakespeare*, 1255–95. Palo Alto: Houghton Mifflin, 1974.

Smyth, Herbert Weir. *Aeschylean Tragedy.* Los Angeles: University of California Press, 1924.

Sophocles. *Antigone.* In *Sophocles: Three Tragedies*, trans. H. D. F. Kitto, 1–45. New York: Galaxy-Oxford, 1964.

———. *Oedipus the King.* In *Sophocles: Three Tragedies*, trans. H. D. F. Kitto, 47–97. New York: Galaxy-Oxford, 1964.

Steiner, George. *Antigones: The Antigone Myth in Western Literature, Art, and Thought.* Oxford: Clarendon Press, 1986.

———. *The Death of Tragedy.* London: Faber & Faber, 1981.

Stone, John A. *Sophocles and Racine.* Geneva: Libraire Droz, 1964.

Vernant, Jean-Pierre. "Ambiguity and Reversal. On the Enigmatic Structure of *Oedipus Rex.*" In *Tragedy and Myth in Ancient Greece*, trans. Janet Lloyd, 87–110. New York: Humanities Press, 1981.

Whitman, Cedric. *Sophocles: A Study of Heroic Humanism.* Cambridge: Harvard University Press, 1971.

Whitmore, Charles. *The Supernatural in Tragedy.* Cambridge: Harvard University Press, 1915.

Winnington-Ingram, R. P. *Sophocles: An Interpretation.* New York: Cambridge University Press, 1980.

Zimmerman, Éléonore. *La Liberté et le destin dans le théâtre de Jean Racine.* Stanford French and Italian Studies, no. 24. Saratoga, CA: Anna Libri, 1982.

5. General: Literary Criticism, Philosophy, Religion

Abrams, M. H. *A Glossary of Literary Terms.* 6th ed. San Diego: Harcourt Brace, 1993.

Babbitt, Irving. *Rousseau and Romanticism.* New York: Houghton Mifflin, 1919.

Bosanquet, Bernard. *A History of Aesthetic.* New York: Macmillan, 1910.

Burkest, Walter. *Greek Religion.* Trans. John Raffon. Cambridge: Harvard University Press, 1985.

Copleston, Frederick. "Aesthetics of Aristotle." In *Greece and Rome. A History of Philosophy: Book One*, 359–71. Vol. 1 of *A History of Philosophy.* New York: Doubleday, 1985.

———. "Hegel (2)." In *Fichte to Nietzsche. A History of Philosophy: Book Three*, 189–225. Vol. 7 of *A History of Philosophy.* New York: Doubleday, 1985.

Countryman, L. William. *The Mystical Way in the Fourth Gospel.* Philadelphia: Fortress Press, 1987.

Danto, Arthur C. "Naturalism." In *Encyclopedia of Philosophy*, ed. Paul Edwards, vol. 5, 448–50. New York: Macmillan, 1967.

Earle, William James. "William James." In *Encyclopedia of Philosophy*, ed. Paul Edwards, vol. 4, 240–49. New York: Macmillan, 1972.

Eliade, Mircea. *The Sacred and the Profane.* New York: Harcourt Brace, 1959.

Fiddes, Paul S. *The Creative Suffering of God.* Oxford: Clarendon Press, 1988.

Guthrie, W. K. C. *The Sophists.* New York: Cambridge University Press, 1971.

Hellwig, Monika K. "Sacrament: Christian Sacraments." In *Encyclopedia of Religion*, ed. Mircea Eliade, vol. 12, 504–11. New York: Macmillan, 1987.

Johnson, Paul. *Modern Times: The World from the 20's to the 80's.* New York: Harper & Row, 1983.

Johnston, William. *The Inner Eye of Love: Mysticism and Religion.* San Francisco: Harper, 1978.

Kasper, Walter. *The God of Jesus Christ.* Trans. Matthew J. O'Connell. London: SCM Press, 1984.

The King James II Version of the Bible. 5th ed. Clinton, MS: Alpha Marketing, 1982.

Krutch, Joseph Wood. *The Modern Temper: A Study and a Confession.* New York: Harcourt Brace, 1929.

Long, Charles H. "Cosmogony." In *Encyclopedia of Religion,* ed. Mircea Eliade, vol. 4, 94–100. New York: Macmillan, 1987.

Luther, Martin. "A Commentary on St. Paul's Epistle to the Galatians." In *Martin Luther: Selections from His Writings,* ed. John Dillenberger, 99–165. New York: Doubleday, 1961.

McCarthy, Charles. "Meditations on August 9, Our Day of Affliction: O Emmanuel!" *The Other Side* (Jan/Feb 1990). 12–13.

McGrath, Alister E. *Luther's Theology of the Cross.* Cambridge, Mass.: Basil Blackwell, 1985.

MacGregor, Geddes. *He Who Let Us Be: A Theology of Love.* New York: Seabury Press, 1975.

Marsh, John, ed. *The Gospel of John.* In *The Pelican New Testament Commentaries.* New York: Penguin, 1983.

Moltmann, Jürgen. *God in Creation.* Trans. Margaret Kohl. San Francisco: Harper & Row, 1991.

Nasr, Seyyed Hossein. *Knowledge and the Sacred.* Albany: State University of New York Press, 1989.

Otto, Rudolph. *The Idea of the Holy.* Trans. John W. Harvey. [1923.] New York: Oxford University Press, 1970.

Plato. *The Republic.* In *The Collected Dialogues of Plato,* ed. Edith Hamilton and Huntington Cairns, 575–844. Princeton: Princeton University Press, 1961.

———. *The Timaeus.* In *The Collected Dialogues of Plato,* ed. Hamilton and Cairns, 475–525. Princeton: Princeton University Press, 1961.

Poe, Edgar Allan. "The Poetic Principle." In *Criticism: The Major Texts,* ed. Walter Jackson Bate, 352–55. San Francisco: Harcourt Brace Jovanovich, 1970.

Raymond, Marcel. *From Baudelaire to Surrealism.* London: Peter Owen, 1961.

Schuon, Frithjof. *The Transcendent Unity of Religions.* Trans. Peter Townsend. London: Faber & Faber, 1953.

Smart, Ninian. *The Religious Experience of Mankind.* New York: Scribner, 1969.

Smith, Huston. "Postmodernism's Impact on the Study of Religion." *Journal of the American Academy of Religion.* 58(4): 653–70 (1990).

———. *The Religions of Man.* San Francisco: Harper & Row, 1986.

Stumpf, Samuel Enoch. *Socrates to Sartre: A History of Philosophy.* 2d ed. San Francisco: McGraw-Hill, 1975.

Thayer, H. S. "Pragmatism." In *Encyclopedia of Philosophy*, ed. Paul Edwards, vol. 6, 430–35. New York: Macmillan, 1972.

Underhill, Evelyn. *Mysticism.* New York: New American Library, 1974.

Wolf, William J. "Atonement: Christian Concepts." In *Encyclopedia of Religion*, ed. Mircea Eliade, vol. 1, 495–98. New York: Macmillan, 1987.

Index